IS GOD A DELUSION?

IS GOD A DELUSION?

What is the evidence?

NICKY GUMBEL

Alpha

with *A Theologian's Perspective*
by Dr Graham Tomlin

ISBN: 978 1 905887 19 4

Scripture quotations taken from the HOLY BIBLE, NEW INTERNATIONAL VERSION.
Copyright © 1973, 1978, 1984 by International Bible Society.
Used by permission of Hodder & Stoughton Publishers, A member of the Hachette Livre UK Group.
All rights reserved.
"NIV" is a registered trademark of International Bible Society.
UK trademark number 1448790.

Published by Alpha International
Holy Trinity Brompton
Brompton Road
London SW7 1JA

Email: publications@alpha.org

Design by James Vincent

Contents

Preface

In March 2007 I attended a debate at Westminster Central Hall on the subject, 'We'd be better off without religion'. Speaking in favour of the proposition were Richard Dawkins, A. C. Grayling and Christopher Hitchens. The hall was packed with over 2,000 people, many of whom had queued for a long time to get in. There was clearly a huge interest in these issues, so I began to read their books and some of the responses.

In October 2007 I gave three talks during our Sunday services, which form the basis of Chapters 1 to 3 of this book. I was conscious that there was some overlap with the first talk of the Alpha course (entitled 'Who Is Jesus?'), in which we examine the evidence for the life, death and Resurrection of Jesus Christ. Rather than trying to merge these talks, I've added 'Who Is Jesus?' as an Appendix for anyone who might be interested.

Revd Dr Graham Tomlin, Dean of St Mellitus and head of St Paul's Theological Centre, kindly agreed to write a response to Richard Dawkins from a theologian's perspective, approaching the same subject from a slightly different angle.

Many thanks to James Orr, Saskia Lawson Johnston, Kitty Kay-Shuttleworth, Sir John Houghton, Geoffrey Locke, Kumar Iyer, Simon Wenham, Alex Guillaume, Ramez Sousou, Randa Hanna, Justin Walford, James Bradley, Jo Glen and Julia Evans for their help and advice on the text.

Chapter One
Has Science Disproved God?

Introduction

Prominent atheists have recently published a number of books. The most well-known is *The God Delusion* by Richard Dawkins, who has been described as 'the nearest thing to a professional atheist since Bertrand Russell'. Others include, *Against All Gods*, by A. C. Grayling, an atheist philosopher; *God is Not Great* by Christopher Hitchens, an atheist journalist; and *Letter to a Christian Nation* and *The End of Faith*, by Sam Harris, an American academic who makes regular TV and radio appearances.

These authors are all atheists on the offensive. Sam Harris believes that all religions are 'both false and dangerous'.[1] Dawkins expands on this idea:

> I think of religion as a dangerous virus. Faith acts like a virus that attacks the young and infects generation after generation. For many people, part of growing up is killing off the virus of faith with a good, strong dose of rational thinking. But if an individual doesn't succeed in shaking it off, his mind is stuck in a permanent state of infancy and there's a real danger that he'll infect the next generation.[2]

> ... Faith can be very, very dangerous and deliberately to implant it into the vulnerable mind of an innocent child is a grievous wrong.[3] ... Horrible as sexual abuse no doubt was, the damage was arguably less than the long-term psychological damage inflicted by bringing the child up Catholic in the first place.[4]

The professed aim of these atheists is to 'eradicate faith', although Dawkins would still allow religion provided it was restricted to 'private acts between consenting adults'. As Harris writes, 'The prospects for eradicating religion in our time do not seem good. Still the same could have been said about the efforts to abolish slavery at the end of the eighteenth century.'[5]

In one sense there is nothing new about this; as the writer to Ecclesiastes says, 'There is nothing new under the sun' (Ecclesiastes 1:9). Christianity has been under attack for two thousand years, yet it has survived and is still growing.[6] There have been numerous attempts to kill off God, with the well-known philosopher Friedrich Nietzsche famously declaring God's death in 1882.[7] But his was not the final word on the matter. A graffiti artist wrote, 'God is dead', signing underneath, 'Nietzsche'. But below it, another graffiti artist wrote, 'Nietzsche is dead', signing underneath, 'God'.

So what is different about the current round of attacks? These atheists have a very clear purpose, so much so that they have even been described as 'purpose driven' atheists. In his book, *The God Delusion*, Dawkins writes, 'If this book works as I intend, religious believers who open it will be atheists when they put it down'.[8] This aggression and vehemence is new to us in the West. People in other parts of the world are more used to aggressive attacks on the basis of religious belief. I was reminded of this on a recent visit to Hungary, which has just emerged from forty years of atheistic communism that tried to eliminate faith. The communist regime attempted to prevent people from bringing their children up as Christians. Jozsef Mindszenty, a Catholic Cardinal who staunchly opposed communism, was imprisoned and tortured. It is perhaps not surprising that the books I have mentioned are not very popular in Hungary.

Nevertheless, these books have attracted a wide readership in the USA, the UK and much of Western Europe. Indeed, in a recent survey of books that MPs were reading during their summer break, *The God Delusion* was high on the list. Clearly, the influence of these works has potential implications on our law, on our education system, ethics, genetics, human rights and our right to bring up our children as Christians. There are important issues at stake.

At the outset, it is worth stating six positive aspects of these authors and their arguments:

1. They are clever people, professors and intellectuals, who use rhetoric, humour and ridicule with skill.
2. Some of the attitudes expressed and attacks made on religion, particularly on violent religion, require courage (on the part of the authors).
3. Some of the attacks on Christianity are well founded and must be taken seriously so that the errors of the past are not repeated.

4. The Christian faith can, and should, benefit from the criticisms of its attackers.

5. These authors have put faith back on the agenda for popular discussion. The apostle Peter says, 'Always be prepared to give an answer to everyone who asks you to give the reason for the hope that you have' (1 Peter 3:5). If issues of faith and religion are being raised at school, at university, in our workplace or around the dinner table, it is important that we have thought through our own response.

6. The conviction that truth matters is a positive move away from relativism, which says *what* you believe does not matter as long as you are sincere. Conversely, these authors say that what you believe *does* matter, because belief affects life. Truth matters. Roger Scruton, an Oxford professor, writes in the *Oxford Dictionary of Epistemology*, 'If anyone tells you that there's no such thing as truth, they're asking you not to believe them, so don't'.[9]

In *The God Delusion*, Dawkins states that, 'The central argument in [the] book' is a chapter entitled, 'Why there almost certainly is no God'. His argument is based upon the premise that science has all but disproved God so people who believe in God are deluded. Dawkins quotes from the dictionary supplied with the Microsoft Word software package, which defines 'delusion' as 'a persistent false belief held in the face of strong contradictory evidence, especially as a symptom of psychiatric disorder'.[10] Dawkins goes on to say, 'The first part captures religious faith perfectly. As to whether it is a symptom of the psychiatric disorder, I am inclined to follow Robert M. Pirsig, author of *Zen and the Art of Motorcycle Maintenance*, when he said, "When one person suffers from a delusion, it is called insanity. When many people suffer from a delusion it's called Religion."'[11]

Is God a delusion? Has science disproved God? Let us consider the evidence by examining three vital questions.

I. Can faith and science live side by side?

Richard Dawkins writes, 'People like to think faith and science can live side by side, but I don't think they can, they are deeply opposed'.[12] What is the evidence for this claim?

According to Dawkins, no sane, intelligent, honest scientist could be a believer because he surmises that all believers are deluded. This implies that if a scientist claims to be a Christian, he or she is either unintelligent (Dawkins describes 'the atheism of the intellectual elite'), or he is insincere, or indeed, insane. He suggests that one of the reasons scientists might claim to believe would be in order to win the Templeton Prize for Religion, which in recent years has been won by leading scientists.

How does this fit with the evidence?

For much of history Christianity and scientific study have been allies, not opponents. This is a well-established fact. Indeed, the Christian worldview provided the right environment for modern science to emerge. The book of Genesis begins, 'In the beginning God created the heavens and the earth' and continues, 'God saw all that he had made, and it was very good' (Genesis 1:1, 31a).

First, it was this belief in one God who created the world that led scientists to expect a world that was ordered, intelligible, rational and uniform. C. S. Lewis encapsulated the reasoning behind this argument thus: 'Men became scientific because they expected Law in Nature, and they expected Law in Nature because they believed in a Legislator'.[13]

Secondly, in the Genesis account God is separate from nature, and creation is essentially good. Belief in a transcendent God (who is separate from nature) means that experimentation is justified. If you believe that the world is evil or you believe in pantheism (that God is in everything), then investigating or doing experiments is risky. However, if you believe in a transcendent God, who created a world that is good but *not* God, then investigation is both legitimate and worthwhile.

Lesslie Newbigin points out, 'In the great cultures of China, India and Egypt, in spite of the brilliant intellectual powers they have manifested, science in the modern sense did not develop'.[14] Professor John Polkinghorne reinforces this point by asserting that the Christian doctrine of Creation 'provided an essential matrix for the coming into being of the scientific enterprise'.[15] As historian Herbert Butterfield writes, 'Science is a child of Christian thought'.[16] When Professor Alister McGrath addressed this point to Richard Dawkins, Dawkins seemed a bit surprised and said, 'That of course could be a historically valid point, but I don't know enough about history to judge'.[17] In a more recent debate between Dawkins and Dr

John Lennox, it was apparent that he has now conceded this point, saying that 'it has to be admitted that of course science grew out of religious tradition'.[18]

History shows that religion was the driving force for science. If you believe that God created the universe, then by investigating the world in a scientific way, you discover more about God through the revelation of himself in creation. This argument can be furthered by considering the views of some of the most prominent scientists of the past.

Nicolaus Copernicus (1473–1543) laid the foundations of modern astronomy and the scientific revolution by suggesting, on mathematical grounds, that the earth travelled around the sun. He held office in the Polish Church as a Canon of Frauenburg Cathedral and described God as 'the Best and Most Orderly Workman of all'.

Galileo Galilei (1564-1642), the mathematician, physicist and astronomer was the founder of modern mechanics and experimental physics. He argued that the earth was not the centre of the universe. Although persecuted by the church, he was a devout Catholic and once said, 'There are two big books, the book of nature and the book of super nature, the Bible'.[19]

Johannes Kepler (1571-1630) was a brilliant early astronomer and mathematician. He was also a deeply sincere Lutheran and said that he was 'thinking God's thoughts after him'.[20]

Robert Boyle (1627-1691), who was a Christian, is renowned as one of the forerunners of modern chemistry and gave his name to 'Boyle's Law'.

Sir Isaac Newton (1642-1727), perhaps the greatest scientist of all time, wrote theological as well as scientific books and he regarded his theological books as more important. He felt that no sciences were better attested than the religion of the Bible.

Michael Faraday (1791-1867) was one of the most brilliant scientists of the nineteenth century, and again the Christian faith was the single most important influence upon his life and work.

Professor James Simpson (1811-1870), the Scottish obstetrician who discovered chloroform, which led to the modern anaesthetic, was once asked this question, 'What's the most important discovery you've ever made?' He replied, 'The most important discovery I ever made was the day I discovered Jesus Christ'.

Louis Pasteur (1822-1895) who discovered the process of pasteurisation and revolutionised microbiology said, 'Science brings us nearer to God'.[21]

Gregor Mendel (1822-1884), Austrian botanist and plant experimenter, whose research into the laws of heredity formed the basis of the modern science of genetics, was a priest, a monk and the Abbot of a monastery, where he did much of his research. The fact that he was a sincere Christian is a problem for Richard Dawkins, as his own scientific field builds on Mendel's work, and Dawkins hails Father Gregor Mendel as the 'founding genius of genetics itself'.[22] However, Dawkins then proceeds to excuse Mendel's faith, writing that, 'Mendel, of course, was a religious man, an Augustinian Monk; but that was in the nineteenth century, when becoming a monk was the easiest way for the young Mendel to pursue his science. For him, it was the equivalent of a research grant.'[23] Thus, Dawkins suggests that Mendel only went into the monastery as a means to carry out free research.

John Cornwell responds to this in his book, *Darwin's Angel*:

> I was unaware that men took the drastic step of entering monasteries in order to enjoy free scientific research funding. Not such a bad idea, though: one square meal a day (albeit frugal), a cell of your own, and endless leisure to pursue those long-term research programmes unencumbered by fleshly distractions. But what farsightedness! Father Mendel came to study plant biology late in his religious life, after seven years' philosophy and theology and a career as a teacher of general subjects.[24]

Joseph Lister (1827-1912) pioneered antiseptic surgery, which has saved thousands of lives. He was a gentle and unassuming man who throughout his life believed himself to be directed by God.

James Clerk Maxwell (1831-1879), the Scottish physicist, best known for his formulation of electro-magnetic theory, is often ranked with Sir Isaac Newton and Albert Einstein for the fundamental nature of his contribution to science. Most modern physicists regard him as *the* scientist of the nineteenth century who had the greatest influence on twentieth century physics. According to Michael Atiyah (Master of Trinity, 1990-91), 'Our modern technological society, from the computer to telecommunications, rests firmly on the foundations established by Maxwell'.[25] Lord Kelvin (William Thomson, 1842-1907), matriculated at the University of Glasgow at the age of ten. He was a professor at the age of twenty-two. The Scottish engineer, mathematician and physicist profoundly influenced the scientific thought of his generation. He was 'foremost among the group of British scientists who helped lay the foundation of modern physics'. He was also a Christian.

All these people were scientists who held strong Christian beliefs. Did scientists only believe in Christianity in the past? What about today? If, as the critics say, science and religion obviously contradict each other, then you would not expect to find any Christian scientists. Yet Dawkins concedes that forty per cent of US working scientists are religious believers. 'In 1916, researchers asked biologists, physicists and mathematicians whether they believed in a God who actively communicates with humankind and to whom one may pray in expectation of receiving an answer. About 40 percent answered in the affirmative.'[26] Nearly one hundred years later, in 1997, the same survey found that the percentage was almost identical.[27] There are many leading scientists today who are believers. Richard Dawkins wittily tries to dismiss British scientists, 'The same three names crop up with the likeable familiarity of senior partners in a firm of Dickensian lawyers: Peacocke, Stannard and Polkinghorne'.[28] But scientists cannot be dismissed simply because their names sound Dickensian! The Revd Dr John Polkinghorne KBE FRS, is a brilliant scientist who was first a Cambridge Professor of Mathematical Physics, becoming Dean and Chaplain of Trinity Hall, Cambridge in 1986 and President of Queens' College Cambridge in 1989. He has written several outstanding books on the relationship between faith (particularly the Christian faith) and science.

Richard Dawkins neglects to mention Sir John Houghton FRS CBE. The leading UK scientist was co-chair of the working group of the Intergovernmental Panel on Climate Change (IPCC) for fourteen years. Houghton was the lead editor of the first three IPCC reports and in 2007 the IPCC shared the Nobel Peace Prize with Al Gore, former US Vice-President. Houghton was Professor in Atmospheric Physics at the University of Oxford, former Chief Executive at the Met Office and founder of the Hadley Centre. He is also chairman of the John Ray Initiative, an organisation 'connecting Environment, Science and Christianity', and he is a founder member of the International Society for Science and Religion.

There are also thousands of scientists in the United States who are Christians. Francis Collins, head of the Human Genome Project is one such scientist. He led a team of over 2,000 scientists, who collaborated to determine the three billion letters of the human genome – our own DNA instruction book. It would take thirty-one years to read those letters aloud. This information is inside every single one of the one hundred trillion cells in our bodies. Each genome contains enough information to fill a library of about five thousand books. If all the chromosomes in a single body were laid out end to end they would stretch one hundred billion miles. Our brains alone have a billion nerve cells. Collins speaks of 'a richly satisfying harmony between the scientific and the spiritual worldviews'.[29] The principles of faith are complementary with the principles of science.

I heard Collins speak at the 2007 National Prayer Breakfast in the United States. He ended his talk as follows:

> To conclude this homily, I propose to do something risky – to ask you all to join me in singing a song. Some may find it ironic that last year's speaker, the rock star Bono, spoke about justice and world economics, but passed up the chance to sing. Now this year's speaker, a scientist who might be considered a bit of a nerd, proposes to sing and play guitar. But the Prayer Breakfast is where we are all supposed to break out of our comfort zones.[30]

He then got up to sing this song:

> Praise the source of faith and learning
> that has sparked and stoked the mind
> With a passion for discerning
> how the world has been designed.
> Let the sense of wonder flowing
> from the wonders we survey
> Keep our faith forever growing
> and renew our need to pray.
>
> God of wisdom, we acknowledge
> that our science and our art
> And the breadth of human knowledge
> only partial truth impart.
> Far beyond our calculation
> lies a depth we cannot sound
> Where your purpose for creation
> and the pulse of life are found.

As two currents in a river
fight each other's undertow
Till converging they deliver
one coherent steady flow;
Blend, oh God, our faith and learning
Till they carve a steady course.
Till they join as one, returning
praise and thanks to You, their source.[31]

Can faith and science live side by side? The evidence suggests that they can.

II. Is there a profound contradiction between science and religious belief?

Richard Dawkins says, 'I'm a scientist and I believe there's a profound contradiction between science and religious belief'.[32]

Before addressing this issue it is worth noting the many disagreements and apparent contradictions within science itself. Conflict between rival scientific views is quite common.

The two main alleged areas of conflicts between science and religion are firstly miracles, and secondly evolution and creation.

1. Miracles

Dawkins follows the philosopher Hume in regarding a miracle as 'a violation of the laws of nature', and consequently he has rejected miracles, suggesting they are impossible.[33] This is a circular argument. If the laws of nature are defined as being impossible to violate, then the supernatural is ruled out from the start and it is impossible to believe in miracles, however strong the evidence.

In 1937, the distinguished German physicist, Max Planck, said, 'Faith in miracles must yield ground, step by step, before the steady and firm advance of the forces of science, and its total defeat is indubitably a mere matter of time'.[34] Planck implied that science now explains that which was once thought to be miraculous, which suggests that those who believed in miracles in the past did so because they did not sufficiently understand the laws of nature. This is not the case. In Jesus' day, everybody knew as well as we do that, for example, it is not 'natural' for a virgin to give birth to a child. They also knew that it was not 'natural' for someone who had been dead for three days to come back to life. If they had not known the laws of nature then they would not have recognised the miracle. As C. S. Lewis writes, 'Belief in miracles, far from depending on ignorance of the laws of nature, is only possible insofar as those laws are known'.[35]

So the real issue concerning miracles appears to be, 'Is there a God?' If there is, then miracles become a real possibility. If God is God, then he created matter, reason, time, space and all the scientific laws; he is therefore at liberty to interfere. If there is no God then miracles are problematic. Philosophy and science alone cannot answer the crucial question of the existence of God. Scientific laws are unlike the laws of pure mathematics that cannot be broken. Rather, scientific laws are descriptive. The term 'miracle', is defined as 'a non-repeatable, counter-instance of an otherwise demonstrable law of nature'.[36]

The problem of miracles arises in *The God Delusion* because Dawkins does not believe they are possible. Thus, he never discusses the evidence for the Resurrection (which will be considered in more detail later). The Resurrection is the linchpin of Christianity – the rational grounds on which Christians believe. Yet Dawkins never considers the Resurrection.

2. Evolution and Creation

The second area of alleged conflict is evolution and the biblical account of creation. As Professor Stephen Hawking (arguably the most brilliant scientist of this generation) has pointed out, any physical theory is only provisional, in the sense that it is only a hypothesis (although, of course, some theories such as the theory of gravity, have a great deal of evidence to support them).

There are different interpretations of Genesis held by sincere Christians. Some Christians believe in a literal six-day creation. Other Christians interpret Genesis 1 differently. They point out that the Hebrew word for 'day' ('yom') has many different meanings, even within Scripture. Since the sun did not appear until day four, the writer probably did not mean literal twenty-four hour days. The word 'yom' can mean 'a long period of time'. Therefore, it is not in conflict with the prevailing scientific view of the vast age of the universe, nor is it in conflict with a gradual evolution in which God not only started the process, but also worked within it to produce a system that culminated in human life. They point out that the chronological order of Genesis 1, written by people with no scientific knowledge, is in some ways similar to that now accepted by evolutionary theorists, with plants appearing first, then animals and then humans.

But what is the purpose (and what is the literary genre) of Genesis? Many Christians prefer to view Genesis 1 as theological rather than scientific, and it is of course poetic in form. Poetic form does not preclude the expression of truth: the truth of a poem is simply different from the truth of a bus timetable. Poetic language can be true without being literally true. When the Psalmist wrote, 'The world is firmly established; it cannot be moved' (Psalm 93:1), he was using a poetic image. Copernicus' opponents made an error when they took this literally and argued that the earth was stationary and that theories of the earth orbiting the sun must therefore be wrong.

Many Christians feel that in the same way, the early chapters of Genesis should not be taken literally. They say that there is strong evidence for macro-evolutionary theory and that it is now accepted by the vast majority of scientists who argue that the fossil evidence is inconsistent with a literal interpretation of the Genesis account. Those who take this view argue that what matters is that it is a God who created and sustains the laws of physics and nature which evolved over time, culminating in human life.

It is clear that there is not necessarily a conflict between science and Scripture. In the light of the uncertainty and different opinions between genuine Christians, it is unwise to be too dogmatic about this issue (certainly if, like me, you are neither a scientist, nor a theologian).

The main point of Genesis 1 is not to answer the questions 'How?' and 'When?' (the scientific questions) but to answer the questions 'Why?' and 'Who?' (the theological questions). The Bible is not primarily a scientific book, but a theological one. It offers a personal explanation more than a scientific one. The scientific explanation does not prove or disprove the personal one, but is complementary. Even Stephen Hawking has admitted that 'science may solve the problem of how the universe began, but it cannot answer the question: why does the universe bother to exist?'[37]

Dr John Lennox uses this illustration:

> Suppose I wheel in the most magnificent cake ever seen and I had in front of me various fellows of every academic and learned society in the world and I picked the top men and I tell them to analyse the cake for me. So out steps the world famous nutritionist and he talks about the balance of the various foods that form this cake. Then a leading bio-chemist analyses the cake at the bio-chemical level. Then a chemist says, 'Well, yes, of course, but now we must get down to the very basic chemicals that form this'. Then the physicist comes on and says, 'Well, yes, these people have told you something, but you really need to get down to the electrons and the protons and the quarks'. And last of all the stage is occupied by the mathematician. And he says, 'Ultimately you need to understand the fundamental equations governing the motion of all the electrons and protons in this cake'. And they finish and it is a magnificent analysis of the cake. And then I turn round to them and I say, 'Ladies and Gentlemen, I've just got one more question for you. Tell me why the cake was made.' And there in

front of them stands Aunt Mathilda who made the cake. It's only when the person who made the cake is prepared to disclose why she's made it that they'll ever understand why. No amount of scientific analysis, however exhaustive and detailed, can answer that question.

And then Aunt Mathilda in the end says, 'I'll let you out of your misery. I've made the cake for my nephew Johnny – it's his birthday next week.'[38]

Dr John Lennox affirms that, 'No amount of scientific analysis of this planet on which we stand will tell you why it was made unless the Creator chooses himself to speak. The fantastic thing is he has spoken and what he has spoken is called Genesis.'[39] There is therefore no necessary conflict between evolution, which attempts to describe the mechanism of creation, and Genesis, which describes the meaning of creation.

The National Academy of Sciences has declared the conflict illusory:

At the root of the apparent conflict between some religions and evolution is a misunderstanding of the critical difference between religious and scientific ways of knowing. Religions and science answer different questions about the world. Whether there is a purpose to the universe or a purpose for human existence are not questions for science. Religious and scientific ways of knowing have played, and will continue to play, significant roles in human history. ... Science is a way of knowing about the natural world. It is limited to explaining the natural world through natural causes. Science can say nothing about the supernatural. Whether God exists or not is a question about which science is neutral.[40]

The Harvard University atheist, Stephen J. Gould, who, aside from Dawkins is probably the most widely read public spokesperson for evolution of the past generation, wrote:

> Science simply cannot by its legitimate methods adjudicate the issue of God's possible superintendence of nature. We neither affirm nor deny it, we simply can't comment on it as scientists ... Darwin himself was agnostic. The great American botanist Asa Gray was a devout Christian. Charles D. Walcott was an equally firm Christian. Either half of my colleagues are enormously stupid, or else the science of Darwinism is fully compatible with conventional religious beliefs and equally compatible with atheism.[41]

Francis Collins writes that, 'There is no conflict in being a rigorous scientist and a person who believes in God'.[42] He therefore concludes that, 'Those who choose to be atheists must find some other basis for taking that position. Evolution won't do.'[43] In saying this, he would be in agreement with perhaps the greatest scientist of all time, Albert Einstein, who said, 'A legitimate conflict between science and religion cannot exist'.[44]

Sir John Houghton writes, 'In trying to argue that science has somehow disproved God, Dawkins and others are going outside the boundaries of what science is about – in fact they are misusing science.... . The view that science tells the whole story is an extremely blinkered one.'[45]

Is there necessarily a profound contradiction between science and religious belief? The evidence suggests not.

III. Is science enough?

Richard Dawkins thinks that every question can be answered by science, but in contrast, Albert Einstein said, 'Science without religion is lame. Religion without science is blind.'[46] He claims that the two are mutually interdependent. In the Bible, the Psalmist says:

> The heavens declare the glory of God;
> the skies proclaim the work of his hands.
> Day after day they pour forth speech;
> night after night they display knowledge.
> There is no speech or language where their voice
> is not heard.
> Their voice goes out into all the earth,
> their words to the ends of the world (Psalm 19:1-4a).

The Psalmist expresses his belief that God has revealed himself in creation. This is then taken further, 'The law of the Lord is perfect, reviving the soul' (Psalm 19:7). We need both scientists to explore God's revelation in creation, and theologians to explore God's revelation in Scripture. Thereby we find the answer to questions that physical sciences alone cannot answer.

The original meaning of 'science' comes from the Latin word 'scientia', meaning 'knowledge'.[47] That is why theology has been regarded as the 'queen' of sciences; she embraces all knowledge. However, Dawkins thinks that theology is not even a subject worthy of study, and that it certainly should not be taught in universities. Yet, theology originally encompassed all the sciences, including the natural sciences on which Dawkins places so much emphasis.

When discussing 'science' in the narrow definition of the word, which is the one Dawkins uses, there are serious questions that science alone cannot answer.

1. How come there is 'something rather than nothing'?[48]

Even atheists concede that we do not know the answer to this question. Sam Harris writes, 'The truth is that no one knows how or why the universe came into being ... . Any intellectually honest person will admit that he does not know why the universe exists.'[49] Dawkins conceded on the Channel 4 programme, *The Root of All Evil*, that, 'Science has not explained the origin of the universe'.[50] The great philosopher Ludwig Wittgenstein said, 'Not *how* the world is, but *that* it is, is the mystical'.[51] Or as Alister McGrath puts it, 'The one inescapable and highly improbable fact about the world is that we, as reflective human beings, are in fact here'.[52] Sir Peter Medawar, an Oxford immunologist who won the Nobel Prize for Medicine, and a self-confessed rationalist (like Dawkins), writes:

> That there is indeed a limit upon science is made very likely by the existence of questions that science cannot answer, and that no conceivable advance of science would empower it to answer ... I have in mind such questions as:
>
> How did everything begin?
> What are we all here for?
> What is the point in living?[53]

This debate can stem from a five-year-old child asking the question, 'Who made God?' In a seemingly more sophisticated way, this is the debate that Dawkins is involved in, which asks the question, 'If you postulate God, who created God?' However, the God that we, as Christians, believe in is not a created God; he is a self-existent God, the one who identifies himself as 'I am who I am'. God is transcendent. The concept of an eternal God who has always been there is certainly difficult to understand. But it is equally very hard to understand what Dawkins proposes – that everything we see has emerged from nothing. We may wish to consider the question: what is easier to believe, that God created something out of nothing, or that nothing created something out of nothing?

Francis Collins writes, 'I cannot see how nature could have created itself. Only a supernatural force that is outside of space and time could have done that.'[54] He goes on to say:

> The major and inescapable flaw of Dawkins' claim that science demands atheism is that it goes beyond the evidence. If God is outside of nature, then science can neither prove nor disprove His existence. Atheism itself must therefore be considered a form of blind faith, in that it adopts a belief system that cannot be defended on the basis of pure reason.[55]

2. How come the universe is so finely tuned?

One of the most extraordinary characteristics about the universe is that it is so finely tuned. Stephen Hawking writes:

> If the density of the universe one second after the Big Bang had been greater by one part in a thousand billion,

the universe would have recollapsed after ten years. On the other hand, if the density of the universe at that time had been less by the same amount, the universe would have been essentially empty since it was about ten years old. How was it that the initial density of the universe was chosen so carefully? Maybe there's some reason why the universe should have precisely the critical density.[56]

The Revd Dr Polkinghorne explains the chances of the universe being so finely tuned:

In the early expansion of the universe there has to be a close balance between the expansive energy (driving things apart) and the force of gravity (pulling things together). If expansion dominated then matter would fly apart too rapidly for condensation into galaxies and stars to take place. Nothing interesting could happen in so thinly spread a world. On the other hand, if gravity dominated the world would collapse in on itself again before there was time for the processes of life to get going.

For us to be possible requires a balance between the effects of expansion and contraction which at a very early epoch in the universe's history (the Plank time) has to differ from equality by not more than 1 in 10^{60}. The numerate will marvel at such a degree of accuracy. For the non-numerate I will borrow an illustration from Paul Davies of what the accuracy means. He points out that it is the same as aiming at a target an inch wide the other side of the observable universe, twenty thousand million light years away and hitting the mark![57]

As Hawking says, 'The odds against a universe like ours emerging out of something like the Big Bang are enormous. I think there are clearly religious implications.'[58]

Richard Dawkins recognises this problem, agreeing that, '... if the laws and constants of physics had been even slightly different, the universe would have developed in such a way that life would have been impossible'.[59] But having ruled out God's intervention, how does he deal with this problem? He concedes that the creation of the universe cannot have just happened, but that perhaps the reason it did happen is that there were lots and lots of attempts. There could have been many instances of the universe expanding and contracting until it got to exactly the right conditions, but he says that science has now discounted that possibility. The other possibility he suggests is that there are billions of universes, and it just so happens that this one has got it exactly right.[60] However, if Dawkins chooses the 'multiverse' hypothesis, what is the evidence that there are billions of universes? Surely this is a theory based on blind faith.

3. How come science cannot meet our deepest needs?

Science is hugely important and valuable. However, if you take a reductionist view of life, reducing life to material and matter, you end up with the conclusion that Dawkins ends with, that life is empty. Dawkins quotes Bertrand Russell, who said, 'I believe that when I die I shall rot, and nothing of my ego will survive'.[61] Katharine Tait, Bertrand Russell's daughter, wrote a book entitled *My Father Bertrand Russell*, and in it she wrote, 'Somewhere at the back of my father's mind and at the bottom of his heart, in the depths of his soul, there was an empty space that had once been filled by God and he never found anything else to put in it'.[62]

Life cannot be reduced to the natural sciences alone. In examining music, Polkinghorne writes, 'The poverty of an objectivistic account is made only too clear when we consider the mystery of music. From a scientific point of view, it is nothing but vibrations in the air, impinging on the eardrums and stimulating neural currents in the brain ... [But] science is not the only way of knowing.' John Humphrys criticises Dawkins' atheism in his book, *In God We Doubt: Confessions of a Failed Atheist*:

> Biologists like Richard Dawkins know a thousand times more than most of us ever will about how our bodies work and how we evolved... . But there is that other mysterious attribute, about which so many scientists are curiously incurious. There is our soul, our spirit, our conscience or whatever else you want to call it... . We are more than the sum of our genes – selfish or otherwise.[63] We sense a spiritual element in that nobility and in the miracle of unselfish love and sacrifice, something beyond our conscious understanding.[64]

Humphrys quotes Giles Fraser, an Anglican vicar who says:

> To marry and make the love commitment is the nearest thing to faith I know because it is something done with the same degree of risk. Couldn't a Dawkins-type figure make a case for love being a fiction, a function of human need, a function of biology and selfish genes?... .There is

something deeply mistaken about thinking love is simply reducible to the chemistry of the brain.[65]

Scientifically, a kiss is no more than the coming together of two sets of lips involving the mutual exchange of carbon dioxide and microbes. But no one would have kissed if that were all there was to it. There is more to a kiss than that and there is certainly more to love than that. The scientific definition does not do justice to a kiss or love or the spiritual world. J. B. Philipps wrote, 'Unfortunately for the scientifically-minded, God is not discoverable or demonstrable by purely scientific means. But that really proves nothing; it simply means that the wrong instruments are being used for the job.'[66]

I was not brought up as a Christian. For many years I was an atheist, and I believed what Richard Dawkins believed (although in a much less sophisticated way). I believed that the world was determined by our environment and by our genes. I thought there was no such thing as unselfish love. It was later in life that, after looking at the evidence for Jesus, I came to put my faith in him. Dawkins says that the only reason why anyone is a Christian is because they are brought up that way. He likens Christian faith to a belief in Santa Claus – something that you may be taught as a child, but which you grow out of as you grow up. But how many people do you know who came to believe in Santa Claus as an adult, having not believed it before? Belief in Christ does not work like that. How does Dawkins explain Christians who convert later in life?

When I came to believe in Jesus, I experienced that there is so much more to life than I had thought before. My faith did not close my thinking; conversely I became much more interested in the world because I suddenly saw it was created by God. My relationship with God gave me a new fascination with the world and led to me valuing it much more. I discovered a newfound value for every human being, because every human being is an individual created by God. My faith gave me a new love for other people and a new desire to do something about the needs of the world. There is nothing greater in this world than to know Jesus Christ, who is the truth, and the one through whom the whole of creation came into being. Reading these books by leading atheists, such as Dawkins, has made me so thankful to be in a relationship with Jesus Christ, to have found a meaning and a purpose to life.

Chapter Two

Does Religion Do more Harm Than Good?

Introduction

On Tuesday mornings at Holy Trinity Brompton church in London, we pray for various groups in the congregation. Recently we met to pray for people who are involved in politics, government and public life. Among the group were four Members of Parliament, two senior police officers, other police officers, Foreign Office staff and civil servants. Talking with them afterwards, it became apparent that these Christians had concerns about working in public life today. One member of the Civil Service said that one of his colleagues, a man in a senior position, is a member of the British Humanist Society and a keen advocate of the views of Dawkins. This man feels that people of faith should be kept out of the Civil Service and he has just been appointed onto the recruitment committee. Recently a Liberal Democrat MP attacked members of the Christian Medical Fellowship, who were giving evidence to the Science and Technology committee, by commenting that what they had to say would be affected by their religious beliefs. Effectively this means that scientific evidence written by Christians could be discounted. In fact, all of our views are affected by our beliefs, whether those beliefs are humanist, atheist, Christian, Muslim and so on.

Many people are experiencing an increasing antipathy towards faith at university, at school and in their professions. A number of people have said that in education, in the judiciary, in the medical profession and in other workplaces, there are situations where it is extremely hard to be a Christian today. It is almost impossible to put Christian beliefs into practice without coming across obstacles. This increase in hostility is relatively new in our society. Tobias Jones, writing in *The Guardian*, said, 'Until a few years ago religion was similar to soft drugs: a blind eye was turned to private use, but woe betide you if you were caught dealing'.[67] The zeitgeist is changing and arguably, possibly for the first time since Constantine in the fourth century, Christians in Western Europe are now on the back foot. No longer is it assumed that the church is a good thing, a benefit to the community. This raises the question, 'Is faith really a good thing, or does it actually do harm?' This debate has huge implications for our society, for the church and for ordinary Christians.

The questions, 'Has science disproved God?', 'Does religion do more harm than good?' and, 'Is faith irrational?' all lead to the fundamental question, 'Is it true?' Richard Dawkins argues that religion is not true and that God is a delusion. Yet he also goes further than this. Some have said to him, 'Okay, it is not true, but surely faith is a good thing because it makes people happier and better, so why not leave people alone?' To this he replies, 'Well, bracing truth is better than false hope', with which we should agree. However, he also goes on to say that faith does not make people better; in fact he believes that 'faith is one of the world's great evils'.[68] Dawkins' Channel 4 documentary on religion was called *The Root of all Evil*. He is particularly scathing about Islam, claiming that the events of 9/11 made him want to stand up and be counted.

Dawkins does not limit his attack to Islam; he vehemently attacks Christianity on the basis that the God of the Bible is an 'evil monster' and that religious people do far more harm than good. Dawkins claims that religion is one of the world's great evils and that consequently to bring your children up in the faith is a form of child abuse. He believes that we need to do everything we can to eradicate religion from our society.

Dawkins' attack is on religion in general, but I want to focus this response to his attack on Christianity; I am neither defending other religions nor am I attacking them.

C. S. Lewis said this:

> If you are a Christian you do not have to believe that all
> the other religions are simply wrong all through. If you
> are an atheist you do have to believe that the main point
> in all the religions of the whole world is simply one huge
> mistake. If you are a Christian, you are free to think that
> all those religions, even the queerest ones, contain at least
> some hint of the truth. When I was an atheist I had to try
> and persuade myself that most of the human race have

always been wrong about the question that mattered to them the most; when I became a Christian, I was able to take a more liberal view.[69]

In response to the question, 'Has the Christian faith done more harm than good?' I would like to start by agreeing with six points made about the potential harm of religion:

1. These self-proclaimed atheists are right to say that some forms of religion can be dangerous and harmful, for example, Satanism, the worship of the devil.

2. They are right to say that terrible things have been done in the name of religion, for example, the attack on the Twin Towers in New York on 9/11.

3. They are right to say that terrible things have been done in the name of Christianity, for example, the Crusades. (The scientist, Francis Collins points out that when talking about 'the hypocritical behaviour of those who profess belief … [we need to] keep in mind that the pure water of spiritual truth is carried in those rusty containers called human beings'.[70])

4. They are right to say that there are some very difficult passages in the Bible, especially in the Old Testament, which are a challenge for us to interpret.

5. They are right to say that there are some forms of religious education that could be abusive.

6. They are right to ask the question, 'Does religion do more harm than good?' Of course this is secondary to the question, 'Is it true?' However, it

is a vital question to ask, because if Christianity does more harm than good then it would be very surprising if it were true. On the other hand, if it does more good than harm, then though that does not necessarily make it true, it does fit with what one would expect.

Let us consider the evidence for these claims and again ask three crucial questions.

1. Is the God of the Bible *really* an 'evil monster'?[71]

Richard Dawkins thinks the biblical God is a monster:

> The God of the Old Testament is arguably the most unpleasant character in all fiction: jealous and proud of it; petty, unjust, unforgiving control-freak, a vindictive, bloodthirsty ethnic cleanser; a misogynistic, homophobic, racist, infanticidal, genocidal, filicidal, pestilential, megalomaniacal, sadomasochistic, capriciously malevolent bully.[72]

As John Humphrys points out, Dawkins has clearly raided the thesaurus for adjectives.[73] As someone else has said, 'Let's hope God doesn't return the compliment!'[74] Of course, there are parts of the Bible, especially parts of the Old Testament, which are extremely difficult to understand and interpret. However, these challenges are not some new scientific discovery. The difficult passages have been there all along and they have been debated before. Let us consider just one example from 200 years ago. In 1795, Thomas Paine wrote in *Age of Reason*, words that are not dissimilar to Dawkins' own:

> Whenever we read … the cruel and tortuous executions, the unrelenting vindictiveness with which more than half the Bible is filled, it would be more consistent that we call it the word of a demon than the word of God. It is a history of wickedness that has served to corrupt and brutalise humankind and for my own part, I sincerely detest it, as I detest everything that is cruel.[75]

So, how do we respond?

1. Examine the evidence of the whole Bible

These atheists are very selective in the passages of the Bible they choose to criticise. For example, the passages in the Pentateuch that Richard Dawkins finds shocking appear alongside others about forgiveness, compassion, hospitality towards strangers and the prohibiting of infant sacrifice. Yet he chooses to ignore them. Dawkins also ignores all the great, prophetic literature, much of which is about social justice and caring for the poor. He ignores the wisdom of the Book of Proverbs and the beautiful poetry of the Psalms. The Bible contains some of the greatest literature in the world – 'insights that continue to shape and nourish the human quest for moral values'.[76]

I have endeavoured to read the whole Bible every year since I have been a Christian (over 30 years), and I simply do not recognise the God that Richard Dawkins describes. I certainly do not believe in the God he describes. The God that I see in the Bible is totally different. He is a God of love, whose love for us is as high as the heavens are above the earth, whose compassion is like that of a parent caring for his children. He is a God of justice and love, a God of kindness and compassion, and a God of mercy and grace (see Psalm 103:11-13).

Reading the Bible is not an academic exercise but the expression of a relationship. Faith is about putting our trust in the God who speaks to us through his Word; God has revealed himself in the Bible. Jesus said, 'You diligently study the Scriptures because you think that by them you have eternal life. These are the scriptures that testify about me, yet you refuse to come to me to have life' (John 5:39).

2. Consider the principles of interpretation

Every form of literature must be interpreted according to its literary genre. When reading literature we need to ask, 'What sort of literature is this – is it history, poetry, or allegory?' Similarly, when reading the Bible, we need to learn to distinguish between literary forms.[77] Not all of scripture is didactic exhortation. Some of it merely records historical events without overtly stating whether such actions were morally 'right' or 'wrong'. Dawkins occasionally mistakes historical record for Christian teaching.[78]

Dawkins seems to think that originally, everybody interpreted the Bible literally, and then when science came along it showed that certain parts could not be interpreted that way, so they began to be interpreted allegorically. However, this is not the case. In the third century, Origen of Alexandria (185-254 AD), interpreted vast parts of the Bible allegorically, far more than we would today. In fact, we would say that the passages he interpreted allegorically were meant to be interpreted literally.

Professor Nicholas Lash, a Roman Catholic writer, says this:

> What I earlier described as Richard Dawkins' fundamentalism in reverse comes through clearly in his curious insistence that the only way to take a biblical text seriously is to believe it literally. To take it allegorically for example is to write it off. Somewhere at the back of all this is a myth that truth can only be expressed through prosaically direct description and that all other literary forms are forms of fiction incapable of expressing truth.[79]

On the matter of interpretation it is also important to understand the principle of progressive revelation. That is, through the Scriptures we gain a greater understanding of what God is like as time goes on, culminating in Jesus Christ. The writer of Hebrews says, 'In the past God spoke to our ancestors through the prophets at many times and in various ways, but in these last days he has spoken to us by his Son ...' (Hebrews 1:1-2). The nature of God is therefore disclosed in Jesus; he is the image of the invisible God (Colossians 1:15) and he is the fulfilment of the Old Testament, the Law and the Prophets.

3. View the Bible through the 'lens of Jesus'

As Christians, we believe that Jesus is the image of the invisible God; Jesus said, 'Anyone who has seen me has seen the Father' (John 14:90). In Luke 24:27, we read that 'beginning with Moses and all the Prophets, he [Jesus] explained to them what was said in all the Scriptures concerning himself'. By looking at the Scriptures through the lens of Jesus, the Old Testament turns into a Christian text. We have to look at the Old Testament through the life, character, death and Resurrection of Jesus. For example, we might consider Jesus' death: Jesus did not do violence, but he allowed violence to be done to him; he gave his life as a ransom for many on our behalf. Many passages in the Old Testament change shape when considered in this way.

We also have to look at the Scriptures through the lens of Jesus' teaching. Jesus said, 'Do to others as you would have them do to you' (Luke 6:31); 'Love your neighbour as yourself' (Matthew 22:39); 'Love your enemies and pray for those who persecute you' (Matthew 5:44). Again, we should interpret the Old Testament through this lens.

We should also remember that Jesus' teaching has been the foundation of our entire civilisation in the West. It has provided a moral code, an absolute right and an absolute wrong, an absolute good and an absolute evil. Richard Dawkins and others like him are turning this on its head. Dawkins writes, 'I have described atonement, the central doctrine of Christianity, as vicious, sado-masochistic and repellent. We should also dismiss it as barking mad.'[80] Similarly Christopher Hitchens thinks that 'the order to "love thy neighbour *as thyself*" is too extreme and too strenuous to be obeyed. ... Humans are not so constituted as to care for others as much as themselves.'[81] In a recent debate, Hitchens went further than this, saying that, 'The deranged idea that we should love our enemies; nothing, nothing, could be more suicidal or immoral than that'.[82]

The problem is that if we are just a product of our genes and our environment, or if we are dancing to the tune of our DNA,[83] then there is no place for absolute standards of morality; there is no absolute right and wrong, no absolute good and evil. Morality becomes purely subjective. Rod Liddle, in his review of *The God Delusion* in the *Sunday Times*, wrote:

> Nowhere though do atheists flail more ineffectually than in attempting to fill what, Sartre called the 'God-shaped Hole' inside all of us: our need to believe in something from which we derive our notion of morality.[84] Atheists squirm when presented with the fact that political regimes that did away with religion and replaced it with a supposedly rational creed (to which the description 'scientific' was frequently appended) ended up murdering more people than Tomás Torquemada (1420-1498) would ever have envisaged. Clearly, something always moves in to fill that gap – and you might argue that the more avowedly 'scientific' it is, the more it will be disposed towards viciousness. Dawkins acknowledges this need for something and concocts 10 commandments. In place of don't kill, steal or covet your neighbour's wife, he has things like, 'Value the future on a timescale longer than your own', or, 'Enjoy your own sex life (so long as it damages nobody else)'. It is the 10 Commandments handed down … not in stone but perhaps on organic tofu. It is beyond parody, and its potential longevity as a useful moral code can be counted in years rather than millenniums.[85]

When the absolute standard is removed, all that remains is utilitarianism; and utilitarian ethics have worrying implications. In the afterword to John Brockman's book, *What is Your Dangerous Idea?* Dawkins wrote this on the subject of eugenics:

> I wonder whether, some sixty years after Hitler's death, we might at least venture to *ask* what the moral difference is between breeding for musical ability and forcing a child to take music lessons. Or why it is acceptable to train fast runners and high jumpers and not to breed them ... hasn't the time come when we should stop being frightened to ask the question?
>
> ... It is harder than most people realise to justify the unique and exclusive status that *Homo sapiens* enjoys (sic) in our unconscious assumptions. Why does 'pro life' always mean 'pro *human* life?' Why are so many people outraged at the idea of killing an eight-celled human conceptus while cheerfully masticating a steak that cost the life of an adult, sentient, and probably terrified cow?[86]

Dawkins thus implies that there is no absolute reason to prefer people to cows. Hitchens often refers to people as mammals. Yet if human beings are not distinguished from animals, the sanctity of human life is abandoned in favour of principles such as, 'It is wrong to reduce the amount of worthwhile life'. Some now argue that it is morally wrong for a mother to *refuse* to abort a 'disabled' child, when he/she could be 'replaced' with a 'normal' child:

> If tests have established that the foetus is abnormal in a way that will drastically impair the quality of its life, it

> will normally be wrong of the mother to reject abortion. ...
> If aborting the abnormal foetus can be followed by having
> another normal one, it will not be wrong to do this. The
> side-effects of abortion will not in general be bad enough
> to outweigh the loss involved in bringing into the world
> someone whose life is much less worth-while than that of
> a normal person who could be conceived instead.[87]

Some take this logic further, saying that we should replace
disabled babies with able-bodied ones.[88] It could even be
argued in some cases that the side effects of killing sick
people could be potentially beneficial; after all, looking after
them is costly and emotionally draining. Yet most people
would recognise that this is abhorrent. It is the very opposite
of Christian morality.

Recently I saw an item on the news about Sister Frances
Dominica who won the Woman of the Year Award in 2007.
Sister Frances started Helen House, which cares for very
sick and dying children, providing practical and spiritual
support for parents and families trying to look after such
children at home.[89] It is deeply moving to see Sister Frances
and the people who work at Helen House caring for these
children with life-threatening and terminal illnesses, in the
most loving way, giving them the best possible life for their
very short period on this earth. It begs the question, 'Why
do they do it?' They do it because they believe in the God
of the Bible and they believe in the sanctity of human life:
that every child, however disabled that child is, is loved by
God, is precious to God, and is made in the image of God.

The God of the Bible as revealed in Jesus Christ is not an evil monster but the only hope for the future of our civilisation.

II. Is faith *really* 'one of the world's great evils'?[90]

Richard Dawkins says, 'I think a case can be made that faith is one of the world's great evils, comparable to the smallpox virus but harder to eradicate'.[91]

Let us consider three aspects of this belief.

1. Distinguish between faith and the misuse of faith

We need to distinguish between faith and the *misuse* of faith. The leading atheists only focus on the misuse of faith, never on its use for good. However, in contrast, when it comes to science, they only focus on its use for good, never on its misuse. Yet science has also been misused throughout history. One need only think of the sinister medical experiments carried out in Nazi Germany, or the terrible weapons developed by science, such as Napalm, landmines, the gas chambers and so on. This misuse is of course atypical of science; but in the same way, so is the misuse of faith. As Cannon David Watson often used to say, 'The opposite of misuse is not disuse, it is right use'.

2. Remember the harm done in the name of atheism

The premise of Dawkins and his colleagues is that if we could only get rid of religion, the world would be vastly improved. Humphrys writes that 'for atheists to claim that without religion peace and harmony would reign is patently absurd. It's not the Bible that proves that. It's the history books.'[92] As Keith Ward points out, 'The two world wars were not fought on religious grounds at all ... there were no religious doctrines or practices at issue in those wars. The most terrible conflicts in human history were not religious.'[93]

Dawkins argues that 'individual atheists may do evil things but they don't do evil things in the name of atheism'.[94] Nobody is suggesting that all atheists do terrible things. My father was an atheist (or, at least, an agnostic), and he was a wonderful man, one of the heroes of my life. But if you look at history, evil things *have* been done in the name of atheism. One example is that of atheistic communism in the twentieth century. Humphrys writes that, 'The greatest horrors inflicted on humanity in the last century were inspired not by religion but by communism'.[95] He quotes the political philosopher John Gray, who makes the point that, 'It is easy to forget how during the twentieth century terror was used on a vast scale by secular regimes. ... "The roots of contemporary terrorism are in radical Western ideology – especially Leninism – far more than in religion".'[96] It is estimated that in the USSR, 20 million were killed; in China: 65 million; North Korea: 2 million; Cambodia: 2 million. It is estimated that the total number of people killed by Communist governments through the extermination of their own population and carrying out explicitly anti-religious policies is somewhere between 85 and 100 million. John Cornwell points out that, 'Stalin's atheism, moreover, was a crucial feature of his entire ideology. He oppressed, imprisoned, murdered [Christians], destroying their ... churches throughout the length and breadth of Russia.'[97] In a speech given on 18 November 1961, Krushchev outlined their philosophy, saying, 'We need a considered and well balanced system of scientific atheistic education which would embrace all strata and groups of the population and prevent the spread of religious views especially among children and adolescents'.[98]

Dawkins says that 'what matters is not whether Hitler and Stalin were atheists, but whether atheism systematically *influences* people to do bad things. There is not the smallest evidence that it does... there is no evidence that his [Stalin's] atheism motivated his brutality.'[99] He goes on even to suggest that his brutality may be motivated by the fact that he had some experience of religion growing up.[100] To which Alister McGrath replies:

> In one of his more bizarre creedal statements as an atheist, Dawkins insists that there is 'not the smallest evidence' that atheism systematically influences people to do bad things. ... The facts are otherwise. In their efforts to enforce their atheist ideology, the Soviet authorities systematically destroyed and eliminated the vast majority of churches and priests during the period 1918 to 1941. The statistics make for dreadful reading. This violence and repression was undertaken in pursuit of an atheist agenda – the elimination of religion.
>
> This hardly fits in with another of Dawkins' creedal statements: '*I do not believe* there is an atheist in the world who would bulldoze Mecca – or Chartres, York Minster or Notre Dame'. Sadly, this noble sentiment is a statement

about his personal credulity, not the reality of things. The history of the Soviet Union is replete with the burning and dynamiting of huge numbers of churches. His pleading that atheism is innocent of the violence and oppression that he associates with religion is simply untenable.[101]

I am not saying that all atheists are communists, or that all atheists fall into the same category. However, the evidence of the twentieth century suggests that the horrors of communism are not logically inconsistent with an atheistic worldview.

3. Appreciate the good done in the name of Jesus

It is sad that Richard Dawkins cannot bring himself to concede that a single human benefit has flowed from religious faith. Mother Teresa is dismissed as 'sanctimoniously hypocritical'.[102] When asked whether he could think of anything, just one positive, even minor thing that religion had done for good, his answer was, 'I really don't think I can think of anything; I really can't'. When asked about great religious art Dawkins replied, 'That's not religion, it is just because the church had the money. Great artists like Michelangelo or Bach and Beethoven would have done whatever they were told to do.'[103]

These atheists go to extreme lengths in their attempt to explain away all the good done in the name of Jesus. For example, Dawkins tries to undermine the faith of political leaders, such as Martin Luther King, the great Christian preacher who did so much to bring racial equality to the United States, by saying that 'their religion was incidental'.[104] He writes, 'Although Martin Luther King was a Christian, he derived his philosophy of non-violent civil disobedience directly from Ghandi, who was not'.[105] But where did Ghandi get his philosophy from? It came partly from Tolstoy, who was a Christian. Where did Tolstoy, Ghandi and Martin Luther King get their philosophy from? They got it from Jesus who said, 'Turn the other cheek' and, 'Love your enemies' (Luke 6:27-29).

Christopher Hitchens takes the same line as Dawkins when writing about Martin Luther King. I was amused by the review of Christopher Hitchens' book in the *Financial Times*:

> The problem with Hitchens' thesis that religion poisons everything is how to explain those who use it to do good. How does Hitchens account for Martin Luther King? Here's how: King was not really a Christian. Really? Well, at no point did King suggest that those who reviled him would be punished in this world or the next. 'In no real as opposed to nominal sense then was he a Christian.'[106]

What about the possibility that King's lack of interest in revenge came from the Gospels? The reviewer goes on to say this: 'I notice that Hitchens doesn't try the King trick on Desmond Tutu. But then Tutu is still alive and we can imagine his response to any suggestion that he is not a real Christian.'[107]

It is not just these great men and women of God that have done good; it is millions of ordinary Christians around the world. Even people who are not Christians themselves recognise the good that is being done in the name of Jesus. John Humphrys is an agnostic and describes himself as a 'failed atheist'. After his programme on Radio 4, *In Search of*

God, he received hundreds of letters in response to his search. He writes:

> For every sceptic, there were dozens of believers who said they had been converted by a specific event or experience ... . They are overwhelmingly sincere people who, one way or another, had found belief in God and that belief has changed their lives ... most of the writers strike me as intelligent, discriminating people who have given a lot of thought to their faith, asked a lot of questions and usually managed to satisfy their doubts ... . For every fanatic there are countless ordinary, decent people who believe in ... God and wish no harm to anyone. Many of them regard it as their duty to try to make the world a better place.[108]

In a recent radio interview, Christopher Hitchens said, 'There is nothing that someone of faith can do that someone without can't do; there are no benefits that a Christian can make to society that a secular person can't also achieve'. After listening to the radio programme, Charlie Mackesy, the artist and sculptor, wrote down the response that he would have given, had he been at the interview:

> All I can say, and I can only speak for myself, Christopher, is that there are things with faith in Jesus that I've done that I'd never have had the courage to do, ever; never had the patience to do; never had the love and the freedom to do; never had the inspiration or the guts to do; and never had the desire to do. I'm sure others without faith could achieve more, much more, but for me, without it, I would never have tried or attempted and failed, sometimes half of

it. Jesus brings life and guts and courage into everything,
for me.[109]

Christians do not claim to be better than those who are not;
simply better than who they would have been, had they not
become Christians.

If we are going to dispute the stated view that religion
does more harm than good, we should look at the evidence
from surveys, which show that committed Christians give
more money to charity; engage in more voluntary work; and
have higher levels of happiness than those of no religion:

> In the *Handbook of Religion and Health* ... authors review
> 2,000 published experiments ... the overall result is that
> religious people tend to live longer and physically healthier
> lives than those who are non-religious. Young religious
> people have significantly lower levels of drug and alcohol
> abuse, criminal delinquency and attempted suicide. Older
> religious people have a stronger sense of well-being and
> life satisfaction. Insofar as any general remarks are in
> order in this area, religion is good for your health![110]

These results are surely what we would expect because Jesus
said, 'I have come that [you] may have life, and have it to
the full' (John 10:10). The Gospel, the Good News of Jesus,
brings freedom and liberation to our lives, and the Holy Spirit
transforms us from within. 'The fruit of the Spirit is love, joy,
peace, patience, kindness, goodness, faithfulness, gentleness
and self-control' (Galatians 5:22-23). We see this fruit in the
lives of people who follow Jesus, in their desire to care for the
poor, visit the prisons, and care for the dying. Can it really be
said that religion is one of the world's great evils?

III. Is Christian upbringing *really* 'child abuse'?

Richard Dawkins has said recently that 'what is really pernicious is teaching children that faith is virtue. Faith is an evil.'[111] In *The God Delusion*, referring to a child who had been sexually abused, he writes that, '... horrible as sexual abuse no doubt was, the damage was arguably less than the long-term psychological damage inflicted by bringing the child up Catholic in the first place'.[112] Of course, if science has disproved God, if God is an evil monster, and if religion is the root of all evil or one of the world's great evils, then of course no one would want to bring up their children as Christians. However, if science has not disproved God; if faith and science are complementary; if the God of the Bible as revealed in Jesus Christ is the supreme example of love (and how we should live our lives). If faith is not some sort of blind leap into the dark believing the impossible, but belief on rational grounds and on good evidence (rather like love); if faith is about a relationship with a person who transforms every aspect of our lives; if becoming a Christian is becoming part of a wonderful community, to which everyone is invited (Jesus said, 'Let the children come to me, and don't hinder them, for the Kingdom of Heaven belongs to such as these' [Matthew 19:14]), then who would want to deprive their children of a Christian upbringing? In fact, it is, in my view, the greatest inheritance we can ever give to our children.

1. Understand the inevitable influence of parents

It is important to understand that all parents influence their children by their life and by their lips. The only way not to have any influence on your children is to have no contact or communication with them. Dawkins is a 'modernist', in that he does not think that he has beliefs. However, of course he does and they come out clearly in his book, *A Devil's Chaplain*. He includes a letter to his daughter, Juliette, which he describes as:

> An open letter to my daughter, written when she was ten. For most of her childhood, I unhappily saw her only for short periods at a time, and it was not easy to talk about the important things of life. I had always been scrupulously careful to avoid the smallest suggestion of infant indoctrination, which I think is ultimately responsible for much of the evil in the world.[113]

He starts his letter, 'I want to write to you about something that is important to me… . Scientists – the specialists in discovering what is true about the world and the universe… .'[114] He then goes on to say what he thinks is true about the world and the universe, which is that Christianity is not true and that there is no evidence for it. The rest of the letter is an attack on religion, an attack on faith and an attack on Christianity; essentially it is anti-religious propaganda. Surely this is also a form of indoctrination; but why is it only abusive to impose religious beliefs on children? To be consistent we must acknowledge that to impose anti-religious beliefs would be equally abusive. There is no 'neutral' gear.

2. Be aware of the dangers of suppressing freedom

Essentially, the atheistic regimes of the twentieth century believed what Richard Dawkins and Christopher Hitchens believe: that God was a delusion; that religion did more harm than good; that religious education was child abuse; and that faith should be eradicated. This is why they made it illegal to teach Christianity to children. Many of those who did teach about the Christian faith were put into prison, and their children were taken away from them. Some Christians were committed to psychiatric hospitals in order to 'cure' them of their delusions.

Therefore, there is a logical path from atheism to doing evil things. This does not mean to say that every atheist will go down this path, but it is important to acknowledge that the path exists. Surely, our society does not want to go down it.

3. Celebrate the benefits of Christian upbringing

I do not know what Richard Dawkins imagines a Christian home to be like, but my experience is that Christian homes are places of (unconditional) love and deep-rooted security. A Christian home is ideally centred around a strong Christian marriage, providing children with a place of safety (with boundaries) where they can build self-confidence, enjoy community and experience freedom. Of course, we should never impose our beliefs on, or indoctrinate our children, but I think there is huge value in teaching children that our own behaviour always has an impact on others, that people matter more than things, that forgiveness is better than revenge. As they grow older, we need to trust them with responsibility and with choice. Naturally we will want to talk to them about our faith but not force it down their throats. We need to avoid any kind of intensity, but we can try to live our faith out as an example to them. As has often been said, children have never been very good at listening to their elders, but they've never failed to imitate them. We have also prayed for our children, that they will never know a time when they have not been walking in a relationship with God.

Conclusion

I used to be an atheist with very similar views, though they were, of course, not as developed as those of Richard Dawkins and Christopher Hitchens. Then I encountered Jesus Christ and discovered a relationship with him: a relationship with the God of the Bible who is not an evil monster. I experienced God's amazing love poured into my heart by the Holy Spirit, which gave me a love for God and a love for other people. That was one of the experiences that led me to become a vicar, because I long for other people to experience that same love in their own lives. Over the years I have seen the impact of this faith on our marriage and family life, and I have seen the impact of Christian faith on other families in our church. I have watched its impact on the young children, the teenagers, the students and young adults who have grown up in a community of faith. Child abuse is the very last expression that would ever come to my mind when talking about a Christian upbringing.

I have also watched people coming to faith in Jesus on our Alpha course at Holy Trinity Brompton, and I have heard many more stories from all around the world. They tell of changed lives: people whose marriages have been restored, whose relationships with their parents or children have changed beyond recognition, people who have been set free from addiction, or who were in prison and have come to faith in Jesus. They speak about how their faith has changed them, and how they are now making a contribution to society. Some have started ministries caring for the poor, for the homeless, and for people with AIDS. Why? Because they have experienced faith in Jesus Christ.

The small things that individual people do – acts of forgiveness, acts of love, acts of service – can be multiplied to millions and millions; they happen each and every day and none of them are necessarily recorded or known about, other than by very few. I cannot speak for religion in general, but I can tell you because I have seen it with my own eyes, that faith in Jesus Christ does not do harm, it does an immeasurable amount of good – because we follow the one who 'went around doing good' (Acts 10:38).

Chapter Three

Is Faith Irrational?

Introduction

Richard Dawkins has said, 'Faith is blind, science is evidence-based.... Science weighs up evidence and advances. Religion is highbound belief for belief's sake.'[115] He defines faith as 'blind trust in the absence of evidence, even in the teeth of evidence'.[116]

Dawkins defines faith as being irrational. However, to start by defining faith as *being* irrational and then to claim that faith *is* irrational is tautology. If you look up the word 'faith' in the dictionary it says that it derives from the Latin word '*fides*', meaning 'trust'. Trust can either be without evidence, or on the basis of evidence. If faith is trust 'in the teeth of evidence' or against evidence, of course it is irrational as Dawkins suggests. Yet equally, if faith is based on evidence then it can be rational. As stated in the introduction, Dawkins proceeds to define faith using the definition of the word 'delusion' from the dictionary supplied with the Microsoft Word software package. A delusion is described as 'a persistent false belief held in the face of strong contradictory evidence'.[117] Therefore, on the basis of Dawkins' definition of faith, faith is a delusion.

The two are interchangeable and synonymous. However, this argument fails if faith is not as Dawkins has defined it. His definition begs the question, 'Is faith in God based on evidence or is it not?' Is faith a delusion?

On a cruise to the Galapagos Islands in May 2007, Dawkins took part in a question and answer session with a group of atheists. He was asked this question: 'What would be the best criticism of your book, *The God Delusion*?' In response Dawkins said, 'I think the best criticism would be any kind of suggestion that there really is good evidence that some kind of supernatural being exists … that would be a good criticism if anybody could come up with one. I think it is revealing that nobody has, and I don't believe anybody could.'[118]

This sets a challenge: is there any evidence for the Christian faith? It is imperative that we seek to answer this question and to give the reason why we believe the critics who say there is no evidence for Christianity today. Let us explore the question, 'Is faith irrational?' by considering five preliminary points about faith itself.

1. Faith is universal

Everyone has beliefs. The existence of God cannot be proved or disproved conclusively. Mathematics is one of the rare disciplines in which there is conclusive proof: $2 + 2 = 4$. In an equation like that there is absolutely no doubt of the truth, no room to argue against it, and therefore no room for faith. In a sense, it is totally arbitrary; the numbers are purely symbolic. As Albert Einstein said, 'As far as the propositions of mathematics refer to reality, they are not certain; and as far as they are certain, they do not refer to reality'.[119]

Even Dawkins concedes that you cannot conclusively disprove the existence of God. It is almost impossible to prove a universal negative. Amy Orr-Ewing, the theologian and Christian apologist, uses the example of a green speckled stone:

> Imagine we were talking about the existence of green spotted stones in the universe today, instead of God. What would I have to do to prove that green spotted stones do not exist? I would have to have an exhaustive knowledge of the universe, an absolute knowledge – that would make you God. What do I have to do to say that green spotted stones do exist? Find one.[120]

Although Dawkins acknowledges that you cannot conclusively prove that there is no God, he declares that it is virtually certain to be the case that God does not exist, and therefore he is an atheist. Nevertheless, this in itself is a belief. Atheists believe that there is no God. Dawkins' belief goes further. As Michael Ruse, the atheist Professor of Philosophy, has pointed out, there is a difference between 'evolution' and 'evolutionism'. Richard Dawkins is an evolutionist and evolutionism is the 'metaphysical or ideological picture built around or on evolution'. Ruse says that evolutionism is 'a religious commitment' and that this is not a 'simple clash between science and religion but rather between two religions'.[121]

Not only do atheists have beliefs, so too do agnostics. A member of our congregation told me this story:

Some time ago, during a slightly alcohol assisted discussion on life, death and the origins of the universe, a friend turned to me and said, 'You're a man of faith, what do you think?'

'We are all men and women of faith,' I replied. 'Some of us have faith that there is a God, some of us have faith that there is no God and neither position is provable.'

'Precisely,' he said. 'That's why I'm an agnostic.'

'You don't escape either,' I replied. 'You just have faith that it's not important to decide.'

Whatever we believe, faith is universal.

2. Faith is an essential part of knowledge

In almost every area of life, faith is an essential part of knowledge. Science itself is a venture of faith. Albert Einstein said, 'The mechanics of discovery are neither logical nor intellectual. It's a sudden illumination, almost a rapture. Later, to be sure, intelligence and analysis and experiment confirm (or invalidate) the intuition. But initially there is a great leap of imagination.'[122]

Similarly, history involves faith. When we read of a historical event we do not have first hand knowledge as we were not there. Instead we have to believe (or not believe) what witnesses and historians tell us.

Legal decisions may require a step of faith. I practised as a barrister for a number of years and am very aware that when a jury brings a guilty verdict it is a step of faith. They do not know that the defendant is guilty; rather they must trust the witnesses and the evidence given. Every verdict involves an element of faith.

Relationships are universal, and they are based on faith. There was a recent article in *The Times* about Miss Yang, the richest woman in China. Miss Yang is worth $16.2 billion (£8 billion) due to the inheritance she received from her father, a former bricklayer, who made this huge amount of money himself. A Hong Kong journalist asked her father why he had handed his fortune over to his daughter. Mr Yang replied, 'Because she's family; I have faith in her'.[123]

Faith is an important part of many aspects of life.

3. For Christians, faith is part of a relationship

For a Christian, faith is about trusting in a person; faith is like love. Faith is not only that which Richard Dawkins supposes it to be – a matter of 'privately entertaining the opinion that a thing called 'God' exists'.[124] Rather, faith is about relationship with a God who has revealed himself in Jesus Christ. Therefore the analogies that the New Testament writers use to describe this relationship are the same terms used to describe the closest personal relationship: the relationship between a parent and a child or a husband and a wife. This relationship of trust transforms our lives, and all of our relationships.

All relationships involve an element of trust. Pope John Paul II said, 'There is no doubt that the capacity to entrust oneself and one's life to another person and the decision to do so are among the most significant and expressive human acts'.[125] Richard Dawkins does understand this in terms of human relationships. In the letter he wrote to his daughter, (which I mentioned earlier) he wrote:

> People sometimes say that you must believe in feelings deep inside, otherwise you'd never be confident of things like, 'My wife loves me'. But this is a bad argument. There can be plenty of evidence that somebody loves you. All through the day when you are with somebody who loves you, you see and hear lots of little tidbits of evidence, and they all add up. It isn't a purely inside feeling, like the feeling that priests call revelation. There are outside things to back up the inside feeling: looks in the eye, tender notes in the voice, little favours and kindnesses; this is all real evidence … . Inside feelings must be backed up by evidence, otherwise you just can't *trust* them.[126]

However, the dictionary likens the word trust to faith. Richard Dawkins is right to say that you can't have *faith* in a person without evidence; all the little pieces of evidence give a basis for trust in human relationships. Yet of course a cynic could dismiss those little bits of evidence, or they could be misinterpreted. Evidence has to be interpreted and it requires trust.

4. Faith and reason can be complementary not contradictory

As previously examined, science and Christian faith are complementary, not contradictory. Similarly, faith and reason can be complementary not contradictory.

Although faith need not be irrational, it may look so from the outside. A nun working as a missionary in the Middle

East was driving her jeep down a road when she ran out of petrol. She did not have a jerry can but she happened to have a potty in the back of the car because of her work with children. So she walked a mile down the road back to the nearest petrol station and filled the potty up with petrol. As she was pouring it into the tank, a Rolls Royce drew up occupied by two wealthy oil sheikhs. They were absolutely fascinated at seeing her pouring the contents of the potty into the jeep. One of them opened the window and said to her, 'Excuse me! My friend and I, although we don't share your religion, we greatly admire your faith!' What they saw looked irrational, but actually there was a very good reason for what she was doing! Similarly, faith may look irrational but our faith in God is based, among other things, on reason.

In the New Testament, in addition to the importance of the heart and the will, there is a strong emphasis on the mind and reason. Jesus said, 'Love the Lord your God with all your heart and with all your soul and with all your *mind*' (italics mine, Matthew 22:37). When Paul was accused of being insane while he was being tried by Festus, he responded, 'I am not insane, most excellent Festus … . What I am saying is true and reasonable' (Acts 26:25). Paul is saying that there is a rational basis for his belief in Jesus and he often spoke about his 'belief in the truth' (2 Thessalonians 2:13). Jesus himself said, 'I am the truth' (John 14:6). To be a Christian is to believe in the truth; there is rationality to faith. As the apostle Peter writes, 'Always be prepared to give an answer to everyone who asks you to give the reason for the hope that you have' (1 Peter 3:15).

So, faith is rational but faith also goes beyond reason. Take, for example, my relationship with my wife, Pippa. If asked whether my love for my wife was rational or irrational, I would want to say that it is not irrational, that there are very good reasons for it, that there is lots of evidence on which I base my love for her. Yet to say that my love for her is merely rational does not do justice to the relationship; a relationship involves more than just the mind; it involves the heart, the soul, every part of our being. There is rationality in relationships, but reason is not enough.

Love, like faith, is far greater and more all encompassing than reason alone. In that sense, faith in God is rational but it is also arational; it is beyond reason and it is greater than reason itself. Pope John Paul II wrote:

> Faith and reason ... each without the other is impoverished and enfeebled ... . Deprived of reason, faith has stressed feeling and experience, and so runs the risk of no longer being a universal proposition. It is an illusion to think that faith, tied to weak reasoning, might be more penetrating; on the contrary, faith then runs the grave risk of withering into myth or superstition. By the same token, reason which is unrelated to an adult faith is not prompted to turn its gaze to the newness and radicality of being.[127]
>
> Faith and reason are like two wings on which the human spirit rises in contemplation of the truth.[128]

Father Raniero Cantalamessa writes:

> A great philosopher from the nineteenth century who was also a believer, Søren Kierkegaard, said that the supreme act of human reason is to acknowledge that there

is something more supreme. It is precisely this leap that many refuse to make. They believe in defending the rights of reason and do not realise that they humiliate and offend reason by negating its capacity to transcend and to project beyond itself.[129]

5. Faith is never forced

Faith is like love; love never coerces, it is never forced. The knowledge of God is promised to those who seek him. Jesus said, 'Ask and it will be given to you; seek and you will find' (Matthew 7:7). God says through Jeremiah, 'You will seek me and find me when you seek me with all your heart' (Jeremiah 29:13). In other words, God does not force himself upon us. The great French mathematical genius, Blaise Pascal, who came to know God through Jesus Christ at the age of thirty-one, pointed out that God has provided enough evidence of himself to convince those of us who have open hearts and minds; but the evidence is not clear enough to convince those who are closed to the idea of God. He wrote:

> Willing to appear openly to those who seek Him with all their heart, and to be hidden from those who flee from him with all their heart, God so regulates the knowledge of Himself that He has given indications of himself which are visible to those who seek him and not to those who do not seek him. There is enough light for those to see who only desire to see, and enough obscurity for those who have a contrary disposition.[130]

So the answer to the question, 'How much evidence is there?' is that there is not enough evidence to be coercive or to force belief, but rather there is enough evidence to make faith rational. The writer of Hebrews defines faith by saying, 'Faith is the *evidence* of things not seen' (italics mine, Hebrews 11:1, King James Version).

Richard Dawkins says, 'No one has come up with any evidence'.[131] However, I want to challenge this assertion. What is this evidence that we base our faith on? It is a cumulative case so let us consider it with a Trinitarian structure.

I. Evidence of God the Creator

The apostle Paul made the assertion that, 'Since the creation of the world God's invisible qualities – his eternal power and divine nature – have been clearly seen, being understood from what he has made' (Romans 1:20).

What is the evidence for this assertion?

1. Evidence from the fact that there is 'something rather than nothing'

Chapter 1 considered how scientists are moving towards a belief that the universe has not always been here and that it began billions of years ago with the 'Big Bang'. 'The existence of the Big Bang begs the question of what came before that, and who or what was responsible.'[132] This view is often unpopular. As Stephen Hawking has written, 'Many people do not like the idea that time has a beginning, probably because it smacks of divine intervention'.[133] If scientists claim that the Big Bang is how the world started it leaves open the question, what caused the Big Bang? Did it come from nothing or was it caused by God?

In the final paragraph of his book, *God and the Astronomers,* the astrophysicist Robert Jawstrow wrote:

> At this moment it seems as though science will never be able to raise the curtain on the mystery of creation … . Now we see how the astronomical evidence leads to a biblical view of the origin of the world. The details differ, but the essential elements and the astronomical and biblical accounts of Genesis are the same; the chain of events leading to man commenced suddenly and sharply at a definite moment in time, in a flash of light and energy.[134]

The key question here is, 'Can you have an uncaused event?' A popular illustration of this is the story of the atheist orator speaking at Hyde Park Corner. He was attacking belief in God and arguing that the world had just happened of its own accord when someone in the crowd hurled a soft tomato, which hit him in the face. Angrily he asked, 'Who threw that?' A Cockney at the back of the crowd shouted out, 'No one threw it, it threw itself!'

2. Evidence from the 'fine tuning' of the universe

As we have seen in Chapter 1, scientists such as Stephen Hawking have shown that, 'Even infinitesimally small differences in the original explosion that cosmologists see as the starting point of our universe would have resulted in a world where conscious life would not occur'.[135] 'According to Robert Jastrow, former head of NASA's Institute for Space Studies, the fine tuning of the universe is "the most powerful evidence for the existence of God ever to have come out of science".'[136]

Sir Roger Penrose, Professor of Mathematics at the University of Oxford, has found that, 'In order to produce a universe resembling the one in which we live, the Creator would have to aim for an absurdly tiny volume of the phase space of possible universes – about one part in 10 to the power of 10^{123}'.[137] Sir John Houghton writes that, 'If all the trees on earth were turned into paper and all the paper covered with zeros to follow the 1, that would be nothing like enough zeros to define that number. If a zero could be placed on every atom in the universe, it would still fall far short of the number of zeros required.'[138] He comments, 'What precision in that fine-tuning! Size, energy and precision – all requiring descriptions beyond our wildest imagination – such is the wonder and magnificence of the universe God has created. Size, energy and precision are Divine characteristics. And for us humans to exist the whole universe is needed with its enormous size and time scale.' [139]

Professor Anthony Flew was a leading atheist for many years, a figurehead of the atheist movement and one of the most influential rationalist atheist philosophers. In 2004, he changed his mind. He did not come to believe in the God of the Bible, but he did come to believe that there must be a God. The reasons for his change of mind were two-fold. First, the fact that the universe has a beginning, and second, the fact that this universe is so finely tuned. 'Flew … abandoned his life-long commitment to atheism and he now accepts that God exists. In his own words he "simply had to go where the evidence leads" and recognise that "the case for God is now much stronger than it was before".'[140]

3. Evidence of the nature of human beings

Dawkins himself must have a sense of right and wrong, else he could not use words like 'good' and 'evil'. However, logically those words cannot be used if it is true that 'there's no such thing as universal good or absolute good or absolute evil'. The philosopher David Hume pointed out that you cannot derive an 'ought' from an 'is'.[141] If things just are, then there cannot be absolute right and absolute wrong. But where does this sense of right and wrong come from? We all have an innate sense of right and wrong – Dawkins himself has this sense. But where does it come from? Paul says that it is the way we are created; God made us with a conscience. He writes that the requirements of the law are written on our hearts and sometimes they accuse and sometimes they defend us; we have a conscience (Romans 2:15).

St Augustine, Bishop of Hippo (354-430 AD), said, 'You [God] made us for yourself and our hearts find no peace until they rest in you'.[142] This is the evidence of experience; the emptiness that is in every human heart. Deep down we know that material things alone cannot satisfy, and that even human relationships are not enough. Bernard Levin (who was a not a Christian), perhaps the greatest columnist of his generation seemed to be only too aware of the inadequate answers to the meaning of life. He wrote:

> Countries like ours are full of people who have all the material comforts they desire, together with such non-

material blessings as a happy family, and yet lead lives of quiet, and at times noisy, desperation, understanding nothing but the fact that there is a hole inside them and that however much food and drink they pour into it, however many motor cars and television sets they stuff it with, however many well balanced children and loyal friends they parade around the edges of it ... it aches.[143]

This is human experience. According to the Encyclopaedia Britannica only 2.5 per cent of the world are atheists. How do we explain the fact that so many people in the world believe in God or are open to the possibility of God's existence?

Dawkins has previously addressed this question with his theory of memes: 'units of cultural inheritance'.[144] He has claimed that religion is a kind of unhealthy virus that has affected practically the whole of humankind. To be fair, Dawkins does not seem to be pushing this so much anymore, because it is a theory for which there is absolutely no evidence. It itself requires blind faith!

In *The God Delusion*, Dawkins says that people only believe because they were brought up that way, which is why he wants to prevent people bringing their children up as Christians. However, upbringing does not solve the question of why so many people believe. A student once said to the great Archbishop of Canterbury, William Temple, 'You believe what you believe because of the way you were brought up'. To which Temple replied, 'That is as may be. But the fact remains that you believe that "I believe what I believe because of the way I was brought up" because of the way you were brought up.'

Dawkins also says that religion is wish fulfilment. This theory goes back to the radical German philosopher, Ludwig Feuerbach, who disliked religion:

> In 1841, Feuerbach argued that God was basically an invention, dreamed up by human beings to provide metaphysical and spiritual consolation. His argument went like this: There is no God. But lots of people believe in God. Why? *Because they want consolation.* So they 'project' or 'objectify' their longings, and they call this 'God'. So this non-existent 'God' is simply a projection of human longings.[145]

Yet as C. S. Lewis pointed out, 'Such wish fulfilment would likely give rise to a very different kind of God than the one described in the Bible'.[146] Just because we wish for something does not mean that it does not exist. For example, human thirst points to the existence of water, which satisfies that thirst. All worldviews including, of course, atheism, are a response to human needs and desires. Wishing for something does not guarantee the existence or non-existence of that something. Someone might wish for a triple-chocolate fudge brownie that contains no calories – it does not exist. Alternatively, I might wish for a drink of water to satisfy my thirst. Human thirst points to the existence of water, which satisfies that thirst. Atheism could be said to be a form of wish fulfilment because something within us wants moral autonomy; we do not like the idea of anyone telling us that certain things are wrong. As some people say, they want to be free to live their own life.

The fact remains that there is this God-shaped hole in every human heart. In reference to this, Pascal wrote that '… the infinite abyss can only be filled by the infinite and immutable object, that is to say, only by God himself'.[147] In other words, there is a God-shaped vacuum in the heart of every human being that cannot be filled by any created thing, but only by God, the Creator, made known in Jesus Christ.

II. Evidence of God the Liberator

As John Stott has written:

> God is partly revealed in the ordered loveliness of the created universe. He is partly revealed in history and in experience, the human conscience, and the human consciousness … . Nevertheless, God's full and final self-revelation … has been given in and through Jesus alone. … 'That is the reason why every enquiry into the truth of Christianity must begin with the historic Jesus.'[148]

1. Evidence of the life of Jesus

Dawkins writes in *The God Delusion*, 'It is even possible to mount a serious, though not widely supported, historical case that Jesus never lived at all'.[149] The reason that this case is not widely supported is because there is a great deal of evidence for Jesus' existence. This comes not only from the Gospels and other Christian writings, but also from non-Christian sources (see Appendix). For example, the Roman historian Tacitus wrote that, 'Christ, from whom they [Christians] got their name, suffered the extreme penalty [ie, the crucifixion] during the reign of Tiberius at the hands of one of our procurators, Pontius Pilate.'[150]

So, there is evidence outside the New Testament for the existence of Jesus. But even if the New Testament did not exist, we would still know these facts about him:

- Jesus of Nazareth was a real person who lived during the rule of Pontius Pilate
- He was a notable teacher
- He gained a reputation as a miracle worker
- Popular opinion about him was divided
- He offended the authorities
- He was executed by crucifixion
- His influence grew rapidly *after* his crucifixion.[151]

We also have the evidence of the New Testament. Richard Dawkins dismisses this, saying that 'All [the gospels] were then copied and recopied, through many different "Chinese Whispers generations" by fallible scribes who, in any case, had their own religious agendas'.[152] This comment suggests a misunderstanding of how textual criticism works. 'Chinese Whispers' involves a message being transmitted through one person at a time. If any one person makes an error in the chain, huge inaccuracies in the message can result. However, multiple copies of the Gospel manuscripts were meticulously made at each point of transmission, so that any errors could be easily identified. In fact, we have over 24,000 manuscripts (see Appendix); there is no ancient document for which we have more manuscripts, nor for which we have copies closer to this, nor for which there are fewer differences between the various ones. Any secular historian would have to concede that we really do know what the authors of the Gospels wrote (for details see Appendix).

In addition, the main evidence for the life of Jesus comes from the Gospels. Richard Dawkins writes that 'the four gospels that make it into the official canon were chosen, more or less arbitrarily...'.[153] This is not true; they were chosen on the basis of apostolicity, universality and orthodoxy. Dawkins also says that 'the only difference between *The Da Vinci Code* and the gospels is that the gospels are ancient fiction while *The Da Vinci Code* is modern fiction'.[154] Albert Einstein was once asked whether he accepted the New Testament as valid historical evidence for the life of Jesus, to which he replied, 'Unquestionably! No one can read the Gospels without feeling the actual presence of Jesus. His personality pulsates in every word. No myth is filled with such life.'[155]

Recent scholarship has shown, using a variety of historiographical techniques, that the authenticity of the *oral* tradition distilled into the Gospels is also very strong. For instance, Richard Bauckham, the distinguished Professor of New Testament at the University of St Andrew's, has argued convincingly that the eyewitnesses to Jesus' life, death and Resurrection remained – throughout their lives – the most recognised and authoritative sources for those traditions about Jesus which the four gospel-writers crystallised into narrative form. In addition, it now appears very probable that the texts of the Gospels are much closer to the way the eyewitnesses actually told their stories than most nineteenth and twentieth century scholars had ever properly appreciated.[156]

2. Evidence of the identity of Jesus

Richard Dawkins says, 'There's no good, historical evidence that Jesus ever thought he was divine'. There are three main pieces of evidence that indicate that Jesus thought he was divine (for further analysis of these claims see Appendix).

First, his teaching centred on himself. Most great religious teachers point away from themselves. Jesus, who was the most humble and self-effacing person, in pointing people to God, pointed to himself. He said, 'Anyone who has seen me has seen God' (John 14:9). Second, there are indirect claims, such as Jesus' claim to be able to forgive sins. The people who saw him forgive sins said, 'Who can forgive sins but God alone?' (Mark 2:7). Third, there are his direct claims, which culminated in the moment when Thomas knelt before him and said, 'My Lord and my God' (John 20:28) and Jesus accepted this. There was also the occasion when Jesus said, 'I and the Father are one' (John 10:30). When the Jews started to stone Jesus, he asked, 'Why are you stoning me?' They replied that they were stoning him for blasphemy 'because you, a mere man, *claim to be God*' (John 10:33, italics mine).

There is good historical evidence that Jesus saw himself as a man whose identity was God. C. S. Lewis pointed out that if it really is the case, then we are left with only three logical possibilities. Firstly, the claims could be true. Secondly, the claims could be untrue, and Jesus knew perfectly well that they were not true, in which case he was an impostor and an evil liar. Thirdly, his claims could be untrue but he did not realise they were untrue, in which case he was deluded.[157]

Richard Dawkins dismisses Lewis' argument suggesting that there is 'a fourth possibility, almost too obvious to need mentioning, that Jesus was honestly mistaken'. Dawkins is saying that Jesus honestly thought he was God but he was not in the third category of being deluded. Of course, you can be honestly mistaken about some things in life and not be deluded or insane. You can be honestly mistaken that you are good tennis player and not be insane; but surely you cannot be honestly mistaken that you are God and not be deluded! The irony of *The God Delusion* is that Dawkins ends up in the position of arguing that to be honestly mistaken that there is a God is a delusion; but to be honestly mistaken that you *are* God is not a delusion. He says that all Christians are deluded because they believe there is a God, but Jesus was not deluded even though he thought he was God. This argument makes no logical sense.

In order to assess which of these three possibilities outlined by C.S. Lewis is right, we need to examine the evidence we have about Jesus' life, his teaching, his character – even Richard Dawkins cannot find fault with Jesus – his fulfilment of prophecy, and of course the Resurrection (see Appendix for detailed examination of this evidence).

3. Evidence for the death and Resurrection of Jesus

Jesus Christ's physical Resurrection from the dead is the cornerstone of Christianity. Yet in *The God Delusion*, Dawkins never even considers the evidence for it. Not to address a case at its strongest is a defect in an argument. It is easy to find things that you can dismiss, but if you are going to dismiss a faith like Christianity, surely you ought to take it on at its strongest point?

For myself, it was through the life, death and in particular the Resurrection of Jesus that I came to believe that there is a God. The world renowned New Testament scholar, Tom Wright, said this, 'The Christian claim is not that Jesus is to be understood in terms of a God about whom we already know; it is this: the Resurrection of Jesus strongly suggests that the world has a Creator, and that that Creator is to be seen in terms of, through the lens of, Jesus'.

What is the evidence that the Resurrection really happened? There are four historical facts that need to be examined (see Appendix):

- Jesus' burial
- The discovery of his empty tomb
- Eyewitness accounts of his post-mortem appearances
- The origin of the disciples' belief in his Resurrection.

Tom Wright concludes his book, *The Resurrection of the Son of God*, by saying that we have to face two facts which, taken together, are extremely powerful:

> We are left with the secure historical conclusion: the tomb was empty, and various 'meetings' took place not only between Jesus and his followers ... but also ... between Jesus and people who had not been his followers. I regard

this conclusion as coming in the same sort of category, of historical probability so high as to be virtually certain, as the death of Augustus in AD 14 or the fall of Jerusalem in AD 70.[158]

Wright goes on to describe the explosion of Christianity that took place around the whole known world and he says, 'That is why as an historian, I cannot explain the rise of early Christianity unless Jesus rose again, leaving an empty tomb behind him'. This is absolutely central because once you come to look at all the evidence that Jesus really was a man whose identity was God, it changes our understanding of what he came to do.

Richard Dawkins believes the cross to be 'vicious, sado-masochistic and repellent. We should also dismiss it as barking mad.'[159] So it would be if Jesus were not God, but as Paul says, 'God was in Christ reconciling the world to himself' (2 Corinthians 5:19). God was in Christ on the cross taking our sins, dying in our place; and it is this that changes people's lives. Paul says in 1 Corinthians that the message of the cross is foolishness to the Greeks; it is foolishness to the scholars and the philosophers, but to us, who have experienced it, it is the power of God. The cross can change our lives and set us free because Jesus Christ came as the liberator.

III. Evidence of God the Transformer

For many people the most impressive evidence for the existence of God is the reality of transformed lives and transformed communities. The apostle Paul wrote, 'We...

are being transformed into his likeness with ever-increasing glory, which comes from the Lord, who is the Spirit' (2 Corinthians 3:18).

1. Evidence of the transformed lives of Paul and the apostles

There is a great deal of historical evidence that the apostles' lives were transformed by what they believed to be an experience of the risen Jesus Christ and the outpouring of the Holy Spirit. Let us consider one example. With astonishing suddenness, Paul, who had been persecuting the church, became the leading advocate of Christianity. What caused this astonishing turn around? Paul was quite clear in his answer – he had seen the once crucified Jesus now risen from the dead, 'Have I not seen Jesus our Lord?' (1 Corinthians 9:1). He lists the early appearances of Christ and then adds '… last of all he appeared also to me' (1 Corinthians 15:8). The evidence of Acts corroborates Paul's claim to have seen the risen Jesus (Acts 9:4 ff; Acts 22:7 ff; Acts 26:14 ff).

Some time ago, two eminent lawyers, both atheists, the Hon George Lord Lyttleton and Gilbert West, were absolutely determined to destroy the Christian faith. They made an agreement between them that the way they would do it would be to undermine two things: the conversion of St Paul and the Resurrection of Jesus Christ.

Lyttleton said to West, 'I'll write a book to prove that Saul of Tarsus was never converted in the way recorded in Acts'. West said, 'I'll write a book to prove that Jesus Christ did not rise from the dead'.

Having written their books they met together. West said to Lyttleton, 'How have you got on?' Lyttleton replied, 'I have written my book, it's called, *Observations on the Conversion and Apostleship of St Paul*. As I have studied the evidence from a legal standpoint, I have become convinced that Saul of Tarsus was converted just the way described in Acts, becoming a radically new man and I have become a Christian. How have you got on?'

To which West replied, 'Well I sifted the evidence for the Resurrection of Jesus Christ from a legal standpoint and I have been satisfied that Jesus of Nazareth was raised from the dead just the way that Matthew, Mark, Luke and John described'.

West's book is called, *Observations on the History and Evidences of the Resurrection of Jesus Christ*. On the fly-leaf he wrote a quotation from Ecclesiastes 11:7, 'Do not find fault before you investigate'. Lyttleton wrote of the evidence of the transformed life of St Paul, 'The conversion and apostleship of St Paul alone duly considered is in itself demonstration sufficient to prove Christianity to be a divine revelation'.[160]

2. Evidence of transformed lives and communities in church history and today

There are so many examples: the conversion of St Augustine, the conversion of Martin Luther, the conversion of Wesley. Personally I have heard innumerable stories of people whose lives have been transformed on Alpha courses at our church and around the world. A typical conversation might go:

'Were you a Christian?'
'No I wasn't.'

'What happened?'

'I encountered Jesus.'

'What difference has Jesus made to your life?'

'Well, he has transformed my relationship with my wife.'
... 'Well, he's set me free from drug abuse.' ... 'He's set me free from alcohol abuse.'

Let me just take one example. Francis Collins, who, as we have seen, is one of today's leading scientists, said this:

I was raised on a small farm in Virginia by ... freethinking parents ... for whom religion was just not very important. ... I became first an agnostic and then an atheist. ... One afternoon, a kindly grandmother with only a few weeks to live shared her own faith in Jesus quite openly with me, and then asked, 'Doctor, what do you believe?'... I fled the room, having the disturbing sense that the atheist ice under my feet was cracking, though I wasn't quite sure why. And then suddenly the reason for my disquiet hit me: I was a scientist. I was supposed to make decisions based on evidence. And yet I had never really considered the evidence for and against faith.

As I explored the evidence more deeply, all around me I began to see signposts to something outside of nature that could only be called God. I realized that the scientific methods can really only answer questions about HOW things work. It can't answer questions about WHY – and those are in fact the most important ones. Why is there something instead of nothing? Why does mathematics work so beautifully to describe nature? Why is the universe so precisely tuned to make life possible? Why do we humans have a universal sense of right and wrong and an urge to do right...

Confronted with these revelations, I realized that my own assumption – that faith was the opposite of reason – was incorrect. I should have known better: Scripture defines faith as 'the substance of things hoped for, the evidence of things not seen'. Evidence! Simultaneously, I realized that atheism was in fact the least rational of all choices. As Chesterton wrote, 'Atheism is indeed the most daring of all dogmas ... it is the assertion of a universal negative'. How could I have had the arrogance to make such an assertion?

After searching for two years more, I ultimately found my own answer – in the loving person of Jesus Christ. Here was a man unlike any other. He was humble and kind-hearted. He reached out to those considered lowest in society. He made astounding statements about loving your enemies. And he promised something that no ordinary man should be able to promise – to forgive sins. On top of all that having assumed all my life that Jesus was just a myth, I was astounded to learn that the evidence for his historical existence was actually overwhelming.

Eventually, I concluded the evidence demanded a verdict. In my 28th year, while hiking in the majestic Cascade mountains, in the Pacific Northwest, I could no longer deny my need for forgiveness and new life – and I gave in and became a follower of Jesus. He is now the rock upon which I stand, the source for me of ultimate love, peace, joy, and hope.[161]

Time after time after time, all around the world, millions of people are experiencing the risen Christ today. This is evidence. It is not just individual lives that have been transformed, but whole communities. The church is evidence. The church has made a difference to the lives of billions of men and women. It has had an impact on society, on culture, on the arts, and on philosophy. We saw, when we looked at science, that the church was the seedbed for the scientific endeavour itself. It has had an impact on family life, on the dignity of human beings, on the rights of children, on care for the poor, for the sick, for the dying and the homeless.

3. Evidence of transformed understanding

C. S. Lewis said, 'I believe in Christianity as I believe in the rising sun'.[162] Not only can you can see the rising sun, but by it you see everything else. Lewis' point was that coming to faith gives a whole new understanding of this world. St Augustine said, 'Credo ut intelligam' (I believe in order that I might understand). This is very similar to the way that science works; you come up with a theory and then you test it with the evidence. It is through belief that we come to understand the world; belief in Jesus, '…in whom are hidden all the treasures of wisdom and knowledge' (Colossians 2:3). Our understanding of this universe comes through faith. This works both ways. In Pope John Paul II's book, *Fides et Ratio* (Faith and Reason), there is one chapter entitled 'Credo ut Intelligam' (I believe in order that I might understand). The next chapter is entitled 'Intelligo ut Credo' (I understand in order that I might believe). In other words, when you come to believe, you don't stop exploring.

Richard Dawkins seems to think that Christians and people who believe in God just stop thinking. Of course, this is simply not the case; when you become a Christian you become more interested in everything and you start exploring, trying to understand more about the universe, which is God's universe. Two examples of how Christian theology helps us to understand the world are the twin doctrines of Creation and the Fall. The doctrine of Creation explains the ubiquity of beauty, that there is something noble about every human being. The doctrine of the Fall explains why nothing is ever quite perfect – both in the created world and also in the human heart. Aleksandr Solzhenitsyn, the great Russian novelist, wrote, 'The line separating good and evil passes not through states, nor between classes, nor between political parties either, but right through every human heart, and through all human hearts'.[163] Faith in God begins to make sense of the world. Faith can make sense of religion, atheism, the human mind, the rational structure of the universe, justice and friendship. Most of all, faith makes sense of love.

If this world has no God, if it just came about, how do we explain love? As Graham Tomlin writes in his postscript, Richard Dawkins' attempt at explaining love is not very satisfactory:

> At the end of the day there is a simple choice to be made. Is love a 'misfiring instinct', an accidental by-product of evolution, and a thinly veiled strategy for personal or genetic survival? Or is it actually the centre of reality, the reason why we are here? Dawkins and Christian faith give

two fundamentally different answers to this question. For Dawkins, love is purely an accident. For Christians, it is the very centre of all that we are. We are made in the image of a God who is love and we were made to learn to love and to be loved. That is the whole meaning of our existence. Christians suggest that we have a deep instinct that tells us that love is no accidental by-product, a 'blessed mistake' but is in fact the very centre of the human experience of human life and happiness.[164]

Conclusion

At the end of each chapter I have written of my own experience, and I want to end this book in the same way. I started out life as an atheist. When I was a teenager I argued against Christianity for a long time. I started to investigate when two very good friends, Nicky and Sila Lee, told me that they had become Christians – they gave me an incentive to look into it. I started to read the New Testament. I didn't read the Gospels as the inspired word of God, I just read them as historical documents. To me they had a ring of truth. I saw that there was evidence for Jesus and I had to make a choice. It certainly was not wish fulfilment because at that moment my thinking was that if it was true and if I was to become a Christian, life was going to be terrible! However, I thought that if it was true, I had to become a Christian. So I said 'yes', thinking that really was the end of all enjoyment of life.

However, the moment I made that step, I experienced the living Jesus Christ, the risen Jesus Christ, and I realised that this was what I had actually been searching for all my life without knowing it, that I had had this God-shaped gap. I wasn't conscious of it, it is just that nothing ever quite satisfied and I was always looking for the next thing to try and satisfy it. When I experienced that relationship with God through Jesus Christ, the longing was satisfied. I experienced God's love for me through the Holy Spirit. It broke my belief that everything we do in life is selfish. I began to realise that if there is a God he can break through with his love and give us a freedom to love that makes such a difference to our lives. This is what I have experienced in the last thirty-three years.

Life is not always easy: there is the dark night of the soul, there are painful experiences of doubt and suffering and all kinds of things that challenge our faith, but at the end of the day my experience has been that there really is good evidence for our faith. Our faith is not irrational; it is rational. It is also beyond rationality because it is a relationship with the God who made us. For me, the key thing is to be able to say, along with the apostle Paul and along with countless others, 'I know whom I have believed' (2 Timothy 1:12).

Postscript

A Theologian's Perspective
By Dr Graham Tomlin

Introduction

Richard Dawkins' *The God Delusion* has been a phenomenon. Taking even its author by surprise, it has outstripped all expectations and has been a runaway best-seller for many months. Ten years ago it was hardly conceivable that a book on religion would achieve such wide coverage. It only shows how much the world has changed in the last decade.

It is worth asking at the outset why Dawkins' book has been so successful. There are a number of possible reasons. First is the 9/11 effect. Ever since the planes crashed into the twin towers on that dreadful day, and it became obvious that this was the work of religious extremists, God and religion have been very public subjects of discussion. Since then, attacks in Madrid, London, Bali, Iraq and other places all over the world have drawn attention to the dangerous phenomenon of religious extremism. We are only too aware that belief in God can make people do all kinds of violent and destructive things and therefore many people are rightly concerned and afraid of the potentially destructive effects of faith within the modern world.

We might think that this suspicion and anger would be directed primarily against extremist Islam, which the media usually portrays as the main origin of religious violence today. However, Christianity has not escaped censure either. Although today it is hard to find many examples of violent Christian extremism, the history of the Christian church is far from unblemished and critics only need to point to the Crusades of the Middle Ages, Medieval anti-Semitism and some more outlandish statements from the weird fringes of Christianity today to lump the Christians in with Al-Qaeda as dangerous fanatics. In that context, a book arguing vehemently against the existence of God and for the harmful effects of religion is bound to have a wide hearing and generate a high level of interest.

The second factor is Dawkins' own reputation. He is of course the Charles Simonyi Professor for the Public Understanding of Science at Oxford University and such a prestigious academic position gives his arguments a certain degree of weight, which they would not have if they came from someone with a less prestigious post. Here is a serious scientist who appears to know what he is talking about when he writes about the progress made by science and how it has apparently eclipsed religion in explaining the world. This is no casual journalist – it is a voice to be taken seriously.

The third factor is the skill of Dawkins' own writing. In previous works such as *The Selfish Gene* and *The Blind Watchmaker*, he has shown himself to be one of the contemporary world's most effective interpreters of science to an unscientific readership. He outstrips most of his contemporaries in his remarkable ability to explain complex scientific matters to those who are not versed in such things.

Perhaps one of the surprising things about Dawkins' book is that its success is in fact founded more upon its rhetoric than its argument. As we shall see, a number of Dawkins' arguments are very questionable and at certain points extremely weak. Yet one thing cannot be disputed, and that is the subtle persuasiveness of his prose. He writes in a flowing, articulate and clever way so that as you read his chapters the very tone of the writing and the skill of the presentation carry the reader along until you are (almost) convinced. It is perhaps slightly ironic that an author and a book which prides itself so strongly on logic and argument in fact depends so much upon rhetoric and persuasion. It is worth reading one of his chapters with an eye to the way the language works, the subtle use of ridicule, the familiar colloquial banter with his reader, and then trying to separate out those from the arguments themselves to see what a brilliant communicator he is. The language quickly creates a cast of goodies and baddies with carefully placed adjectives and pejorative language ('Christian zealots', 'Bible-believing fundamentalists', 'decent liberals', 'thoughtful sceptics' etc).

However, in this short response I want to look at some of the key arguments Dawkins makes and suggest how a Christian might answer them. Many people will have read Dawkins and be a little puzzled as to how he might be answered from a Christian perspective. Others will not have read Dawkins but will have had conversations with friends who have, and will perhaps have been troubled as to whether Dawkins' arguments really do spell the end of faith and the demise of God. Whether you have read Dawkins or not, this short piece aims to help you think through the strength of his arguments and perhaps question whether they are as compelling as they can sometimes initially seem.

1. No sign of God?

One of Dawkins' key arguments is very simple; that there is simply no compelling evidence for the existence of God, especially when it comes to analysing God's supposed intervention in the world. If God answers prayer, performs miracles and the like, then we ought to be able to tell that he is doing such a thing - there simply should be more obvious evidence for him.

Dawkins is impatient with the argument of Stephen Jay Gould that science and religion are 'Non-Overlapping Magisteria'. Dawkins is not convinced by the idea that science and religion are dealing with two separate types of reality, and really have nothing to say to each other, that they are answering different questions and therefore are mutually exclusive. Gould argues that God is somehow so far beyond this world that science cannot analyse him and his dealings and therefore we should not expect to be able to discern God's hand within the world. Dawkins, however, argues that this does not make sense if religious people really do claim that God intervenes in answer to prayer or performs miracles.

So how might a Christian respond to this? In a sense Dawkins has a point. If God does intervene within the world on particular occasions that seem to transcend the normal operation of physical and biological processes, then we might expect to be able to tell when he does so. However, Dawkins is, by his own admission, no theologian, and does not really appreciate a Christian view of miracles. It is bad theology as well as bad science to imagine a 'God of the gaps' where God is invoked to explain anything that science cannot. This is because God is not a 'thing' within the world that causes other 'things' to happen according to the normal observable physical laws of nature. On a Christian understanding, miracles are not random interventions of God, like a secret visitor moving chess pieces on a board while the players are not looking. Miracles are instead actions, which seem to obey a different set of laws, or operate in another dimension of reality that is not specifically accessible to scientific analysis or study, or which show up in odd events in our own world. As the Princeton philosopher Diogenes Allen puts it:

> In certain unusual situations such as creating a chosen people, revealing divine intentions in Jesus, and revealing the nature of the Kingdom of God, higher laws come into play that give a different outcome than normal physical laws which concern different situations. The normal physical laws do not apply because we are in a domain that extends beyond their competence.[165]

God usually achieves his purposes *indirectly*, through human agency. Particular people in the Bible or Christian history are normally the agents of miracles, whether it be Moses parting the Red Sea, Jesus raising the dead, or Christian saints performing healings. Christian theology says that God is both beyond this world (transcendent) and yet also operates within this world (immanent). If God is the Creator of this physical world and yet occasionally acts within it, through ordinary (or perhaps extraordinary) people, according to a different order of things, then we would expect to see occasional events and experiences within our world which are hard to explain under natural terms. These would include what many people describe as religious experience, inexplicable healings in response to prayer and indeed countless incidents every day around the world which seem unlikely but which are attributed to the fact that someone prayed. None of these can ever be proved to be a direct intervention of God because they are immune to scientific proof – they don't obey the normal patterns of interaction between physical bodies observable by science. However, such apparently inexplicable events give a sign of the Christian belief that one day God will bring about a new heaven and a new earth, where this different order of things will be apparent for all to see. Miracles for the Christian are not random, isolated acts of capricious divine choice, but they are signs of another reality. They are signs of the Kingdom of God which, one day, will come.

Dawkins himself gives a tantalising hint of this towards the end of *The God Delusion*. In the final chapter, he draws attention to our very limited imagination, due to the particular way in which we have evolved. He writes:

> Our brains are not equipped to imagine what it would be like to be a neutrino passing through a wall, in the vast interstices of which that wall 'really' consists. Nor can our understanding cope with what happens when things move at close to the speed of light. ... Evolution in Middle World ill equipped us to handle very improbable events. But in the vastness of astronomical space, or geological time, events that seem impossible in Middle World turn out to be inevitable.[166]

In other words, Dawkins hints that there could be a different order of things from this one. Might it be, for example, that the resurrected Jesus (who of course we are told appeared capable of walking through walls!) might be a picture of that future, who came into our world at a specific moment of history to reveal to us the new heaven and the new earth that one day God will bring about?

In short, if Dawkins is asking for cast-iron proof of miracles that meet all the requirements of scientific certainty, then neither he nor anyone else will ever find them. But the reason is not that miracles do not happen, it is simply that they belong to another dimension of reality that is beyond our current capacity to discern. Miracles will always seem to us inexplicable events, which are open to a number of different interpretations. The unbeliever will want to hold onto his faith that one day they will be explained in some naturalistic way. The Christian will see them as signs of a different order of things altogether: the Kingdom of God.

2. Bad arguments for God?

Dawkins spends quite some time looking at the various arguments that have been used for the existence of God and trying to show that they simply do not work. He makes a decent fist of the point; however it is hamstrung by his lack of knowledge of the subtleties of Christian theology. This is one of the frustrating aspects of the book. It would be irritating for a biologist if I were to try to write a book about science in which I displayed my ignorance of the meaning of multicellularity, or the behaviour of chromosomes. So you can imagine it is a little annoying to read Dawkins writing about a subject of which he is certainly no expert and not just a little uninformed.

For example, Dawkins tries to present some of the classic arguments for the existence of God, such as Thomas Aquinas' proofs, as supposed knock-down arguments to convince the sceptic that God exists.[167] However, as many theologians have pointed out, Aquinas' arguments for the existence of God, such as the Ontological Argument, the Teleological Argument and the Argument from Design, were never meant to be hard and fast proofs to the non-believer to convince them that God exists. Aquinas presents them (as do most other mainstream Christian theologians) as confirmations of faith, rather than proofs of it. In other words, for those who have a belief in God, they provide a rationale for showing how that belief makes sense. They show how believing in God interprets the rest of reality and how the world looks from the standpoint of faith in God. Aquinas knows that no one can be argued into belief in God, it is something that emerges in quite another way – by God's own initiative and a human response to it. Dawkins criticises these arguments for failing to do something that they never set out to achieve in the first place.

Another argument that Dawkins seeks to undermine is the argument from personal experience, the argument that, 'I experience the reality of God, therefore he exists'. Dawkins delights in pointing out all kinds of examples of supposed religious experiences that have turned out to have a completely naturalistic explanation. Of course, it is possible to do this time and time again. There are many experiences that we have, or that others profess, which on closer examination turn out to have a perfectly simple naturalistic explanation or which have simply been misinterpreted. Having said that, it is still very hard to argue away the whole of religious experience from human history along these lines. Experience of the divine or a dimension beyond the physical is pervasive in just about every culture that has ever lived on the face of the planet. Of course it is interpreted in different ways but the bare fact remains that countless people profess to an experience of something beyond the material or the natural, which the naturalist can always try to explain away, but finds it hard to do so because of the sheer mass of such testimony.

A further point is that very often it seems that experiences that we attribute to God's intervention often seem to involve natural means. I heard a story recently of a Christian girl who was in deep distress after the loss of a very close relation, and who cried out to God for an answer, for meaning and for comfort. She was, as it were, giving God a last chance to reach her. At that very moment another Christian came up to her on a deserted beach, put his arms round her and just gave her a big hug. This was someone she knew and the action was not entirely out of character, but the circumstances of his being there at that particular moment were unusual and somewhat remarkable. Now of course it is possible to interpret this as just a chance event that this person happened to be walking along at that moment and performed that gesture. Naturally, however, and perfectly justifiably, she would interpret this as an answer to her prayer and that this gesture was a sign of something much greater – in other words, the love of God for her, not just the love of this human being. Very often, what we call a 'religious experience' occurs when we interpret what might otherwise be seen as a natural event in supernatural ways because of the particular timing or emotions that surround the event. In Christian understanding, God usually uses people to do his work for him. He has created a world in which he has appointed us humans, out of all the species of the world, to care for creation and to care for each other. Therefore what we might interpret naturally can, from a Christian point of view, also be evidence of God's care and love for us.

The third argument that Dawkins likes to ridicule is Pascal's 'Wager'. Pascal was a seventeenth century Christian philosopher who wrote an Apology for the Christian religion, in a famous section of which he argued that it was better to bet on God's existence than his non-existence. His argument was that, as Dawkins put it, 'You'd better believe in God, because if you are right you stand to get eternal bliss and if you are wrong it won't make any difference anyway. On the other hand, if you don't believe in God and you turn out to be wrong you get eternal damnation, whereas if you are right it makes no difference.'[168]

Now it is of course fairly easy to poke holes in this argument as Dawkins himself does (I won't rehearse the arguments here).[169] The key point, however, is that Pascal did not promote this as an argument for believing in God. The argument has a different function for Pascal. He is trying to show that the real reason why unbelievers don't believe is because they simply don't want to. As he famously says elsewhere in his *Pensées*, 'It is the heart and not our reason which is decisive'.[170] His argument in 'The Wager' is directed at his sophisticated gambling friends in seventeenth century Paris. He simply wants to point out to them that if they were true betting men, looking for the best odds, they would always bet on God because the odds are far more in favour of belief than they are of unbelief. But he goes on to point out that his friends do not believe, which only goes to show that their reasons for unbelief are not based on the logical odds that might be available in this question, but come from another source. They don't believe simply because they don't want to believe. So again, this argument was not and never can be presented as a fail-safe argument for the existence of God.

Christian theology has always claimed that faith does not emerge from a process of argument. It can be aided by careful thinking, but it emerges when people encounter

God for themselves at a much deeper level than the merely rational. Therefore, arguments for the existence of God can only ever be confirmations or explorations of the internal coherence and consistency of faith rather than something presented to unbelievers to convince them. That is not to say that good arguments cannot be suggested that would point towards belief, but they can only ever hope to show the internal coherence of belief in God rather than providing 100 per cent proof to force the unbeliever into submission.

3. Science explains everything?

Dawkins argues that natural selection explains everything we can see around us and therefore there is no need for God. When the French philosopher Laplace explained his ideas to Napoleon, and the emperor asked him the question, 'Where is God in your philosophy?' Laplace is supposed to have famously replied, 'I have no need of that hypothesis'. The main point of Dawkins' argument is that the existence of complex beings such as ourselves can be perfectly explained by the process of natural selection and there is really no need for supposing any kind of God as part of the process. Natural selection can show how complex human beings can emerge from very simple elements. Therefore, the Argument from Design does not work, and we can do without God. He also goes on to argue that the existence of God is extremely improbable. The direction of evolution is always from something very simple towards something very complex. If a God were placed at the beginning of the process, you would still be left with the question of how that very complex being (God) came into being in the first place. It is a slightly more sophisticated version of the old argument that simply asks the question 'Well, who made God then?'

Dawkins may well be right in arguing that natural selection does provide a good explanation of how we have developed from very simple organisms, how life emerged, and how the world has come to be what it is today. However, there remain a number of questions. For example, several philosophers have pointed out that it is hard to imagine human language appearing through a simple process of genetic evolution. Evolutionary process would normally expect a new ability to have appeared in one individual first; however, it is impossible for language to be individual – it has to involve at least two people who converse together. There is also a further question that Dawkins is simply unable to answer and that is the question of why there is anything here at all. Yes, the process may have begun with some very simple elements combining to form life, but why were those elements there in the first place? He cannot escape the question of the origins of life by simply positing a set of chemical entities that combined to form life.

Now this is the argument of infinite regress, where you have to find some kind of starting point for the whole process. The Big Bang is of course one possible solution to this argument, but even that does not provide an answer because it still leaves open the question, why there was something to go 'bang' in the first place? The problem is that viewed within a naturalistic framework, everything we see has a prior cause to it, and it is logically very difficult to find an original first cause within that naturalistic structure. We need something outside the system, which precisely by being outside the system needs no prior cause to launch the whole thing in the first place. Christian theology has always claimed God to be transcendent – in other words, not contained within the discernable and analysable world. He is, in a sense, outside the system although, as we have seen already, he does act in other ways than through physical agency, not least in the Incarnation of his own self in the person of Jesus Christ. Therefore, God does not have to be as simple as Dawkins argues; he would only need to be simple if he were part of the naturalistic world, part of the continuum of space and time that we experience as the universe.

The basic problem is that biology can explain something of how we came to be what we are today, but it cannot explain everything, or most importantly the existence of anything in the first place. Given certain basic elements, biology can explain the process by which we emerged and evolved, but it cannot explain the origins of those very elements themselves. Christian theology suggests that these elements, the stuff from which life emerged, must have come from a non-naturalistic source, in other words, a being beyond this world who gave rise to them. It seems to me perfectly compatible with the story of Genesis to argue that the world originates in the will of a good and loving Creator who made a world out of nothing, which was initially simple but which developed over time. The account in Genesis 1 allows for development and evolution because it builds time into the process of creation. God did not create the world in one instant but, as the story tells us, it emerged over time (the mythical period of seven days). Even at the end of the creation narrative there is a sense that the world is still to develop, with it needing to be filled, subdued and nurtured by humankind. Natural selection is not a disproof of God. It is simply a description of how life develops. Therefore, there is no contradiction between believing in evolution and arguing for a non-naturalistic theistic explanation as a starting point for the world as we see it.

Furthermore, it is hard on the purely naturalistic explanation to argue for the intelligibility of the universe. Why does the universe make sense? Why is it not entirely random? If the world is explicable then that itself requires some justification or explanation. In other words how is science possible? Intelligibility cannot arise from coincidence. Christians would argue that the existence of God does not so much explain the gaps in our knowledge as explain the fact that knowledge is possible in the first place. If the world is the creation of a rational and intelligible being then it makes sense that it is a rational, intelligible place. If it emerged instead from the chance convergence of a number of chemical elements then it is hard to see why it contains any intelligibility at all.

4. Religion a mistake?

One of the more curious parts of Dawkins' argument is his account of the origins of religion. This concerns his well-known idea of 'memes' or 'units of meaning', which are transferred like a virus from one mind to another and spread in the same way that a virus does. This provides an account of the origins of religion that fits with natural selection, so that 'memes' are like genes that ensure their own survival by mutating to create different forms. Units of ideas or 'memes' will adapt to new circumstances and replicate themselves in subtle and ingenious ways to ensure their survival.

This argument has been criticised on a number of occasions. It is interesting to see that Dawkins seems to be less sure of it now and it takes a much less central place in his quiver of arrows than it used to. The basic problem is this: who is to say which 'meme' is a good virus or a bad virus? He has already come to the conclusion that religion is a bad thing and therefore he explains its origins through this metaphor of a disruptive virus. However, who is to say whether religion is a virus or whether Dawkins' own ideas are a virus which is spreading in the same way? There is also of course no independent, objective proof of the existence of 'memes'. It is really a metaphor he is using rather than a scientifically proven fact. This is rather strange as he accuses Christians of basing their faith upon things that are not proven, and so it is a little bit rich to see him arguing so strongly for such an idea himself. The existence of 'memes' is assumed and unquestioned and one might direct the same arguments towards them as he does towards God. Another thing: if religion is a mistaken accident, a biological error, presumably it would have been quickly discarded by the process of evolutionary development. The fact that it has persisted so stubbornly and strongly suggests either that it has a different origin, or that it is hard-wired into us as something lasting and valuable.

Dawkins suggests that religion arises from very simple people misinterpreting ordinary, naturalistic events. He uses an example of a group of South Sea islanders who worshipped a strange figure called John Frum, which evolved into an extreme devotion to the Duke of Edinburgh. The implication of course is that devotion to Jesus emerged from a similar kind of na ve wrong-headedness. The difficulty here is his rather patronizing assumption that first century people were extremely gullible and liable to believe in the unlikely possibility of someone rising from the dead. As many New Testament scholars have pointed out however, first century people did not believe that a man could re-appear after he had died any more than we do. In fact, the Resurrection of an individual was the exact opposite of what first century Jews expected. They were expecting some kind of Resurrection at the end of time but the last thing anyone was looking for was the Resurrection of a particular individual in time. This went against all their expectations and so it is very unlikely that they would have naively accepted such a story unless there were compelling reasons for doing so. The origins of faith in the resurrected Jesus cannot be explained quite as simply as Dawkins hopes.

5. Goodness is an accident?

Dawkins realises that he also has to come up with some explanation for the origins of morality and goodness if he is to complete his case against religious belief. Again, as in the idea of 'memes', he goes for a naturalistic explanation that fits in with evolutionary biology. He argues that there are Darwinian reasons for people to be generous or kind towards each other; for example, favouring the fortunes of one's own kin, reciprocity where 'if you scratch my back I'll scratch yours', the benefits of gaining a reputation for generosity and so on. However, this does not get away from the basic implication here that all our behaviour is ultimately selfish. It ensures the survival of our own genes and our own selves. Even altruistic behaviour is only altruistic on the surface; underneath it is a thinly disguised means of personal or genetic survival. Dawkins has to argue that love as we understand it is a result of genetic misfiring, an accidental, instinctive by-product of our desire to save and replicate our own genetic features. At the same time, he also argues that we have an instinctive knowledge of good and evil and therefore we do not need to be told it by God or the Bible or the church or anything like that. There are a number of significant problems with this approach.

    a. As we saw in the last point, again there is a real problem of evidence. This is simply a suggestion that Dawkins has come up with, but going by his own rules we should not believe anything that does not have a strong evidential backing. This argument is precisely an example of the very thing he is accusing his opponents of. How are we to take seriously an argument that has as little evidential basis as this?

b. Christian faith is not so much about telling us what is right and wrong as about enabling us to do what it is right and to avoid what is wrong. In one sense the Bible does not contain much that is new or distinct from any other religious traditions in its understanding of what is right and wrong. Murder, lying, theft and greed are bad. Kindness, generosity, love and friendship are good. So the point of Christian faith is not to give us some new information on what is right and wrong which cannot be discerned from any other means (although there are some distinct characteristics of Christian morality which do mark it off in some respects from other moral schemes). Rather, Christian faith is about enabling us to follow the path of goodness. It describes how we might find a relationship with our Creator restored through his intervention into human life through his Son Jesus Christ. It describes how God's own power, the Holy Spirit, can enter a human life, give that life a new dimension of energy and purpose to do what is right, and to live a good life; to live according to the Kingdom of God. Criticising Christian morality for not offering a distinct list of dos and don'ts that cannot be found elsewhere is simply to miss the point.

c. At the end of the day there is a simple choice to be made. Is love a 'misfiring instinct', an accidental by-product of evolution and a thinly veiled strategy for personal or genetic survival? Or is it actually the centre of reality, the reason why we are here? Dawkins and Christian faith give two fundamentally different answers to this question. For Dawkins, love is purely an accident. For Christians, it is the very centre of all that we are. We are made in the image of a God who is love and we were made to learn to love and to be loved. That is the whole meaning of our existence. Christians suggest that we have a deep instinct that tells us that love is no accidental by-product, a 'blessed mistake', but is in fact the very centre of the human experience of human life and happiness.

6. The tyrant of the Bible?

Dawkins offers us an amusing and ribald description of the God of the Bible, arguing that such a character is by no means a being worthy of worship and devotion, but is, in fact, a cruel tyrant, best confined to history and thrown out of all civilized discussion. True, it is not hard to make this case by careful selection of passages, especially from the Old Testament and by the careful ignoring of others where God is presented as long-suffering, patient, 'Slow to anger and abounding in love and faithfulness' (Exodus 34:6). Although Dawkins ridicules the God of the Bible along these lines, he is strangely silent about Jesus, seeing him as some kind of exception to the ugly character he thinks he sees from the pages of the Bible.

Dawkins again shows his ignorance of Christian theology by taking an over-literalistic reading of the texts. He fails to see that in Christian theology there is a clear interpretative criterion for reading the Old Testament, and that is that we read the Old Testament in the light of Jesus Christ. The central clue the Bible gives us to the character of God is in Jesus. That is the place we should look first and we should interpret everything else in the light of him. The character of Jesus reflects the character of the God of the Old Testament – patiently kind, endlessly loving, achingly compassionate, angry at evil, fiercely loyal. God desires us to worship him not because he is some insecure despot who demands that we cravenly bow down before him, but because for us to worship a God who is in himself love, is in fact the best thing we can do. We worship God not because he needs it but because it is good for us.

Moreover, Dawkins again suggests a rather inadequate and weak argument for how morality arises. He suggests that the 'zeitgeist' or 'spirit of the age' creates morality, or in other words, that a general consensus emerges within particular societies as to what is good and what is bad, and we should follow that, rather than any account from any sacred text (and certainly not the example of the despotic God he sees in the Old Testament). The difficulty here is that the zeitgeist is notoriously malleable. The moods of particular societies are easily influenced by powerful figures with money and influence who can engineer all kinds of malicious outcomes. The classic example of course is the zeitgeist of Germany in the 1930s, where the general consensus of opinion was that it was perfectly legitimate to oppress and exterminate Jews, gypsies, enemies of the Nazi party and the like. What if the zeitgeist of a particular culture decided that it was acceptable to sacrifice children (as in ancient Near Eastern religion) or to encourage paedophilia (as in Graeco-Roman culture) or for wives to throw themselves on the funeral pyres of their husbands (as in Indian life for many centuries)? Should that zeitgeist therefore be followed? Or is it the case that we do, after all, need something external to the general consensus of opinion within any given culture, that gives us a model of what human life is meant to be and how it is to be lived?

7. The evil of Religion?

One of the main planks of Dawkins' argument and that of the many other atheists is the suggestion that religion makes people do very bad things. Whereas moderate, gentle atheists like himself are incapable of doing anything nasty to anyone, religion, being rooted in a transcendent cause, has the power to make people do unspeakably evil things to each other and the world in which they live. Of course it is not hard to find examples of this in the past or from the contemporary world. Much of the violent conflict in the world today from Iraq to Palestine, and terrorist attacks in the USA and Europe, is due, at least in some part, to religion.

Dawkins takes this argument a step further when he responds to those who ask him why he is so vehemently opposed even to moderate religion. It might seem hard for him to argue that a gentle vicar in a country parish in England is implicated in the gravest evil in the world today; however, this is precisely the argument he makes. His point is that moderate religion provides a kind of 'cover' for the bad things done by extremists in religion. If the moderates in religion gave up their faith then it would expose the extremists for who they are and would deprive them of a vital source of potential support.

Of course Dawkins has a point that religion can make people do bad things, but then again, so can almost anything that is important to human beings. People have done unspeakably horrible things to each other in the name of their family, tribe, nation, football team, or even in the name of love. To seek to eliminate anything that can be used for violent ends would logically mean eliminating each of these along with religion. The evils of the early and middle decades of the twentieth century were largely caused by utopian visions of political change or nationalistic purity. They had very little to do with religion but far more to do with race and ideology. Ethnic cleansing in the Balkans, Rwanda and Burundi was carried out in the name of tribal superiority rather than any specifically religious motivation. Dawkins is surprisingly confident that atheism would never sponsor such destruction. However, it is estimated that Josef Stalin was responsible for the deaths of 20 million people in Russia in the 1930s-50s. Despite Dawkins' brief protestations to the contrary, Stalin's programme for reform in Russian was explicitly atheistic, including its determination to eradicate religion in all its forms. It also had deep roots in Stalin's own desire to replace God with himself: as Nikolai Bukharin, Stalin's colleague once said of him, 'He cannot help taking revenge on people, on all people, but especially those who are in any way better or higher than he'.[171] Mao Zedong's attempts to create an explicitly atheistic society in the 'Great Leap Forward' and the Cultural Revolution were similarly responsible for the deaths of tens of millions of Chinese in the 1960s-1970s.

Atheism is just as capable as religion (if not more) of dastardly acts of violence and oppression. The point here is not that religion is necessarily superior to atheism in this regard, it is simply to say that human beings are such that they are likely to take any idea, however good or bad, and turn it into an excuse for doing violence to each other. In fact this insight points very clearly to a Christian understanding of human nature that is both gloriously optimistic and hugely pessimistic. Christians believe that we are made in the image of God, capable of amazing acts of love, compassion, mercy and grace. Yet we are also deeply flawed, fragile and fallen, equally capable of acts of terrible evil. This seems to fit the human condition and the course of history far better than the overly optimistic suggestions of atheists such as Dawkins.

Moreover it is possible to turn this same point about moderate religion back on Dawkins' view of atheism. Moderate, non-violent atheism such as Dawkins' own could also be argued to provide 'cover' for militant, violent atheism as that espoused by Stalin, Mao and others. Some of Dawkins' own rhetoric calling for the eradication of religion and the criminalisation of bringing up children as religious could be argued to be inflammatory and pointing in one sure direction: the persecution and oppression of Christians, Muslims and Jews. Living in a world of frequent religious and ethnic tension it is hard to see how Dawkins' aggressively condemnatory language can do anything else but foster hatred and cruelty towards religious people, which is every bit as unpleasant as the acts of which he accuses Christians.

8. The inspiration of atheism?

Dawkins rounds off his book with a warm and cuddly vision of the future where atheism will provide consolation, inspire the imagination and bring about a world of harmony, peace and love. It is clearly an attempt to steal the clothes from religious claims to provide consolation and strength in a difficult world and to answer the charge that atheism strips the world of its wonder and glory. Can atheism provide such hope? Can it provide the way forward for a glorious future for humanity?

The difficulty here is finding any evidence that this might ever be the case. Previous experiments in trying to build an avowedly atheistic society that deliberately tries to get rid of religion are not very promising. Soviet Russia, as we have seen, was not exactly a beacon of tolerance, peace and harmony (at least not for the 20 million who died). Nor were Pol Pot's Cambodia, Mao's China or the state of Burma today. In other words atheism has so far failed in every attempt to provide this perfect society that Dawkins so optimistically thinks will emerge.

Now of course it is possible to accuse Christianity of failing in the same way. Atheists might argue that Christians have equally failed to provide and to create the perfect society. However, Christians never claim to be able to do this. They always claim that until the coming of the new heavens and the new earth, this world will always be imperfect with its characteristic mixture of good and evil. As St Augustine put it, the City of God will live uncomfortably alongside the City of the World in this present age, and so we are not to expect to see the perfect society before God brings it about. Atheism has no belief in any other dimension than the physical and natural, in other words, what you see is what you get – there is nothing more. For atheism therefore, either the perfect society can be created here and now under the conditions of time and history, or it is a chimera, a hopeless dream. Christians say quite bluntly that we will never create the perfect society here on earth. That has to wait until God's creation of a new heaven and a new earth. We get glimpses of that kingdom now in our experiences of justice, mercy, forgiveness and the presence of God but they are only that – glimpses, and not the full reality.

Richard Dawkins reminds me of someone passionately convinced of the virtues of sight, confronted by people trying to explain to him the concept of smell. Such a person might be absolutely committed to the view that vision alone can understand and explain reality. If sight is all we need, if it can contain, explain and describe the whole of reality, then why on earth would we need smell? It cannot be anything real and must be a figment of other people's imaginations. This person cannot grasp an aroma with her eyes, and therefore concludes that it does not exist. And as a result she misses out on a vital dimension of reality. She has to deride those who claim to smell things from time to time as deluded and pathetic. Vision is such a magnificent thing that she cannot see why anyone would want anything else. One day these poor misguided 'smellers' will come to see the truth that what they claim is just an illusion, a mistake.

Perhaps the main problem with Dawkins is that he starts the discussion in the wrong place. Nowhere does the Bible show any interest in the question, 'Is there a God?' The writers do not try to prove it, demonstrate it or argue for it. They simply assume it. This is the only way God can be found. Dawkins tends to think belief in God is like a random opinion that one happens to hold, just like believing that it will rain tomorrow, or that there are Yetis in the Himalayas. Yet 'faith' in the Bible is much richer and stronger than that, and involves much more than a mere idea. Faith begins when I realise that I am not what I might be. In fact, to be blunt, I am self-centred, thoughtless, loveless and need to change. And I need to find a way to do that. The God of the Bible is not interested in whether we happen to entertain the opinion that he exists nor not. He is interested in changing us. And only those prepared for that challenge will ever find him.

We find him when we begin to live life on the assumption that not only is God there, but he is to be counted on. We find him when we live on the assumption that Jesus Christ is the exact image of God, and that the point of life is to let God transform us to be like him. We find him when we begin to live as if every person we meet is valuable because they are made in God's image; that there is always hope in the worst situation because Jesus rose from the dead; that the Bible is God's Word through which he wants to speak to us each day. In other words, faith involves personal risk, and only those prepared to take that risk can find God.

Jesus told a story about a man digging in a field, who found a box of hidden treasure, and who sold all he had to buy that field. God hides himself in our world, just as the treasure is hidden in the field. He is not obvious, but waits to be found by those who are serious enough to stake everything on him, 'sell everything they have' to follow him. Of course it is possible to look at this world and miss God altogether. Jesus Christ said, 'Those who seek will find' (Luke 11:9). God is searching for us and is there to be found but only by those who risk everything to do so. Those who do find him find love, adventure and satisfaction beyond what they imagined possible.

Appendix
Who Is Jesus?

Introduction

For much of my life I have not been a Christian. My father was Jewish by race and agnostic by conviction. My mother was not a churchgoer. I was at times an atheist and at times an agnostic, unsure of what I believed. I had studied the Bible in religion classes at school, but had ended up rejecting it all and arguing against the Christian faith. On Valentine's night 1974, my convictions were challenged by my greatest friend Nicky Lee. I had just got back from a party when Nicky and his girlfriend, Sila (now his wife) appeared and told me that they had become Christians. I was horrified! I had come across Christians in my year off and was deeply suspicious of them, in particular their propensity to smile so much.

I knew I had to help my friends so I thought that I would embark on some thorough research of the subject. I happened to have a rather dusty copy of the Bible on my shelves, so that night I picked it up and started reading. I read all the way through Matthew, Mark and Luke, and halfway through John's Gospel. I fell asleep. When I woke up, I finished John's Gospel and carried on through Acts, Romans, and 1 and 2 Corinthians. I was completely gripped by what I read. I had read it before and it had meant virtually nothing to me. This time it came alive and I could not put it down. When I finished reading the New Testament, I came to the conclusion that it was true.

I spent ten years studying law and practising as a barrister, so for me evidence is very important. I could not have taken a blind leap of faith, but was willing to take a step of faith based on good historical evidence. In this chapter I want to examine some of this historical evidence.

I am told that in an old communist Russian dictionary Jesus is described as 'a mythical figure who never existed'. No serious historian could maintain that position today. There is a great deal of evidence for Jesus' existence. This comes not only from the Gospels and other Christian writings, but also from non-Christian sources. For example, the Roman historians Tacitus (directly) and Suetonius (indirectly) both write about him. The Jewish historian Josephus, born in AD 37, describes Jesus and his followers thus:

> Now there was about this time, Jesus, a wise man, if it be lawful to call him a man, for he was a doer of wonderful works – a teacher of such men as receive the truth with pleasure. He drew over to him both many of the Jews, and many of the Gentiles. He was [the] Christ; and when Pilate, at the suggestion of the principal men amongst us, had condemned him to the cross, those that loved him at first did not forsake him, for he appeared to them alive again the third day, as the divine prophets had foretold these

and ten thousand other wonderful things concerning him; and the tribe of Christians so named after him, are not extinct at this day.[172]

So there is evidence outside the New Testament for the existence of Jesus. Furthermore, the evidence in the New Testament is very strong. Sometimes people say, 'The New Testament was written a long time ago. How do we know that what they wrote down has not been changed over the years?' The answer is that we do know very accurately, through the science of textual criticism, what the New Testament writers wrote. Essentially the shorter the time span between the date the manuscript was written and the earliest available copy, the more texts we have, and the higher the quality of the existing texts, the less doubt there is about the original.

The late Professor F. F. Bruce (who was Rylands professor of biblical criticism and exegesis at the University of Manchester) shows in his book *Are the New Testament Documents Reliable?* how wealthy the New Testament is in manuscript attestation by comparing its texts with other historical works. The table below summarises the facts and shows the extent of the evidence for the New Testament's authenticity.

Work	When written	Earliest copy	Time span (yrs)	No. of copies
Herodotus	488-428 bc	ad 900	1,300	8
Thucydides	c. 460-400 bc	c. ad 900	1,300	8
Caesar's Gallic War	58-50 bc	ad 900	950	9-10
Livy's History of Rome	59 bc-ad 17	ad 900	900	20
New Testament	ad 40-100	ad 130 (full manuscripts ad 350)	300	5,000+ Greek 10,000 Latin 9,300 others

F. F. Bruce points out that for Caesar's *Gallic War* we have nine or ten copies and the oldest was written some 950 years later than Caesar's day. For Livy's *History of Rome* we have not more than twenty copies, the earliest of which comes from around AD 900, though none of these are complete. Of the fourteen books of Tacitus' *Histories* only twenty copies survive; of the surviving sixteen books of his *Annals*, ten portions of his two great historical works depend entirely on two manuscripts, one of the ninth century and one of the eleventh century. The history of Thucydides is known almost entirely from eight manuscripts belonging to c. AD 900. The same is true of Herodotus' *Histories*. Yet no classical scholar doubts the authenticity of these works, in spite of the large time gap and the relatively small number of manuscripts. As regards the New Testament, we have a great abundance of material. The New Testament was committed to writing between AD 40 and AD 100. We have excellent full manuscripts for the whole New Testament dating from as early as AD 350 (a time span of only 300 years), papyri containing most of the New Testament writings dating from the third century and even a fragment of John's Gospel which scientists have carbon-dated to around AD 125. There are over 5,000 Greek manuscripts, over 10,000 Latin manuscripts and 9,300 other manuscripts, together with more than 36,000 citings in the writings of the early church fathers. As one of the greatest ever textual critics, F. J. A. Hort, said, 'In the variety and fullness of the evidence on which it rests, the text of the New Testament stands absolutely and unapproachably alone among ancient prose writings'.[173]

F. F. Bruce summarises the evidence by quoting Sir Frederic Kenyon, a leading scholar in this area:

> The interval then between the dates of original composition and the earliest extant evidence becomes so small as to be in fact negligible, and the last foundation for any doubt that the Scriptures have come down to us substantially as they were written has now been removed. Both the *authenticity* and the *general integrity* of the books of the New Testament may be regarded as finally established.[174]

Albert Einstein was once asked whether he accepted the New Testament as valid historical evidence for the life of Jesus, to which he replied, 'Unquestionably! No one can read the Gospels without feeling the actual presence of Jesus. His personality pulsates in every word. No myth is filled with such life.'[175]

So there is persuasive and plausible evidence for the strength of the *textual* tradition. But recent scholarship has shown, using a variety of historiographical techniques, that the authenticity of the *oral* tradition distilled into the Gospels is also very strong. For instance, Richard Bauckham, the distinguished Professor of New Testament at the University of St. Andrew's, has argued convincingly that the eyewitnesses to Jesus' life, death and Resurrection remained – throughout their lives – the most recognised and authoritative sources for those traditions about Jesus which the four gospel-writers crystallised into narrative form. In addition, it now appears very probable that the texts of the gospels are much closer to the way the eyewitnesses actually told their stories than most nineteenth and twentieth century scholars had ever properly appreciated.[176]

We know, then, from different types of evidence both outside and inside the New Testament that Jesus existed. But who is he? I heard Martin Scorsese say on television that he made the film *The Last Temptation of Christ* in order to show that Jesus was a real human being. Yet that is not the issue at the moment. Few people today would doubt that Jesus was fully human. He had a human body: he was sometimes tired (John 4:6) and hungry (Matthew 4:2). He had human emotions: he was angry (Mark 11:15-17), he loved (Mark 10:21) and he was sad (John 11:35). He had human experiences: he grew up in a family (Mark 6:3), he had a job (Mark 6:3), he was tempted (Mark 1:13) and he experienced suffering and death (Mark 15:15-40).

What many say today is that Jesus was *only* a human being – albeit a great religious teacher. Dan Brown's book *The Da Vinci Code* suggests that Jesus was not the Son of

God but a mortal prophet, a great religious teacher and a powerful man of staggering influence. On the other hand, Bono, the lead singer of U2 has said, 'I believe that Jesus *is* the Son of God. I do believe it, odd as it sounds.' Even Jean-Jacques Rousseau, one of the greatest philosophers of the Enlightenment, was convinced that, 'If the life and death of Socrates are those of a sage, the life and death of Jesus are those of a god'.[177] Can we agree with such statements? What evidence is there to suggest that Jesus was more than just a man of staggering influence or a great moral teacher? The answer, as we shall see, is that there is a great deal of evidence. This evidence supports the Christian contention that Jesus was and is the unique Son of God, the second Person of the Trinity.

I. What did he say about himself?

Some people say, 'Jesus never claimed to be God'. Indeed, it is true that Jesus did not go round wearing a t-shirt saying, 'I am God'. Yet when one looks at all he taught and claimed, there is little doubt that he was conscious of being a person whose identity was God.

1. Teaching centred on himself

One of the fascinating things about Jesus is that so much of his teaching was centred on himself. Most great religious teachers point away from themselves and to God - indeed we would expect them to: Muhammad would have been horrified at the suggestion he was divine; the Buddha claimed anyone in principle could follow him in attaining 'nirvana'; Plato believed that if he could perceive his world of 'ideal forms', many others could too. But Christianity is not an '-ism', because it is not about an idea. It is about a person: Jesus, the most humble and self-effacing person who ever lived, in pointing people to God, pointed to himself. He said, in effect, 'If you want to have a relationship with God, you need to come to me' (see John 14:6). It is through a relationship with him that we encounter God.

There is a hunger deep within the human heart. The leading psychologists of the twentieth century have all recognised this. Freud said, 'People are hungry for love'. Jung said, 'People are hungry for security'. Adler said, 'People are hungry for significance'. Jesus said, 'I am the bread of life' (John 6:35). In other words, 'If you want your hunger satisfied, come to me'.

Addiction is a major problem in our society. Speaking about himself, Jesus said, 'If the Son sets you free, you will be free indeed'. Many people are depressed, disillusioned and in a dark place. Jesus said, 'I am the light of the world. Whoever follows me will never walk in darkness, but will have the light of life' (John 8:12). For me, when I became a Christian, it was as if the light had suddenly been turned on and I could see things for the first time.

Many are fearful of death. One woman said to me that sometimes she couldn't sleep and that she would wake up in a cold sweat, frightened about death, because she didn't know what was going to happen when she died. Jesus said, 'I am the Resurrection and the life. Those who believe in me will live, even though they die; and whoever lives and believes in me will never die' (John 11:25-26). Mother Teresa was asked shortly before her death, 'Are you afraid of dying?' She replied, 'How can I be? Dying is going home to God. I've never been afraid. No. On the contrary, I'm really looking forward to it!'

Many people are not sure how to run their lives or who they should follow. I can remember, before I was a Christian, that I would be impressed by someone and want to be like them, but before long it would be a different person, and then another. Jesus said, 'Follow *me*' (Mark 1:17). He said to receive him was to receive God (Matthew 10:40), to welcome him was to welcome God (Mark 9:37) and to have seen him was to have seen God (John 14:9). A child once drew a picture and her mother asked what she was doing. The child said, 'I am drawing a picture of God'. The mother said, 'Don't be silly. You can't draw a picture of God. No one knows what God looks like.' The child replied, 'Well, they will do by the time I have finished!' Jesus said in effect, 'If you want to know what God looks like, look at me'.

2. Indirect claims

Jesus said a number of things, which, although not direct claims to be God, show that he regarded himself as being in the same position as God, as we will see in the examples that follow. Jesus' claim to be able to forgive sins is well known. For example, on one occasion he said to a man who was paralysed, 'Son, your sins are forgiven' (Mark 2:5). The reaction of the religious leaders was, 'Why does this man talk like that? He's blaspheming! Who can forgive sins but God alone?' Jesus went on to prove that he did have the authority to forgive sins by healing the paralysed man. This claim to be able to forgive sins is indeed an astonishing claim.

C. S. Lewis puts it well when he says in his book *Mere Christianity*:

> One part of the claim tends to slip past us unnoticed because we have heard it so often that we no longer see what it amounts to. I mean the claim to forgive sins: any sins. Now unless the speaker is God, this is really so preposterous as to be comic. We can all understand how a man forgives offences against himself. You tread on my toes and I forgive you, you steal my money and I forgive you. But what should we make of a man, himself unrobbed and untrodden on, who announced that he forgave you for treading on other men's toes and stealing other men's money? Asinine fatuity is the kindest description we should give of his conduct. Yet this is what Jesus did. He told people that their sins were forgiven, and never waited to consult all the other people whom their sins had undoubtedly injured. He unhesitatingly behaved as if He was the party chiefly concerned, the person chiefly offended in all offences. This makes sense only if He really was the God whose laws are broken and whose love is wounded in every sin. In the mouth of any speaker who is not God, these words would imply what I can only regard as a silliness and conceit unrivalled by any other character in history.[178]

Another extraordinary claim that Jesus made was that one day he would judge the world (Matthew 25:31-32). He said he would return and 'sit on his throne in heavenly glory' (v. 31). All the nations would be gathered before him. He would pass judgment on them. Some would receive an inheritance prepared for them since the creation of the world and eternal life, but others would suffer the punishment of being separated from him for ever. Jesus said he would decide what happens to every one of us at the end of time. Not only would he be the Judge, he would also be the criterion of judgment. What happens to us on the Day of Judgment depends on how we respond to Jesus in this life (Matthew 25:40, 45). Suppose you overheard a man walking down the street with a megaphone shouting, 'On the Day of Judgment you will all appear before me and I will decide your eternal destiny. What happens to you will depend on how you've treated me and my followers.' For a mere human being to make such a claim would be preposterous. Here we have another indirect claim to have the identity of Almighty God.

When Jesus was asked, 'Are you the Christ, the Son of the Blessed One?' Jesus said, 'I am . . . and you will see the Son of Man sitting at the right hand of the Mighty One and coming on the clouds of heaven'. The high priest tore his clothes. 'Why do we need any more witnesses?' he asked. 'You have heard the blasphemy. What do you think?' (Mark 14:61-64). In this account it appears Jesus was condemned to death for the assertion he made about himself. A claim tantamount to a claim to be God was blasphemy in Jewish eyes, worthy of death. On one occasion, when the Jews started to stone Jesus, he asked, 'Why are you stoning me?' They replied that they were stoning him for blasphemy 'because you, a mere man, *claim to be God'* (John 10:33, italics mine). His enemies clearly thought that this was exactly what he was declaring.

When Thomas, one of his disciples, knelt down before Jesus and said, 'My Lord and my God' (John 20:28), Jesus didn't turn to him and say, 'No, no, don't say that; I am not God'. He said, 'Because you have seen me, you have believed; blessed are those who have not seen and yet have believed' (John 20:29). He rebuked Thomas for being so slow to get the point!

If somebody makes claims like these they need to be tested. There are all sorts of people who make all kinds of claims. The mere fact that somebody claims to be someone does not mean that they are right. There are many people, some in psychiatric hospitals, who are deluded. They think they are Napoleon or the Pope, but they are not. Jesus claimed to be the unique Son of God – God made flesh. There are three logical possibilities. If the claims were untrue, either he knew they were untrue – in which case he was an imposter, and an evil one at that. That is the first possibility. Or he did not know – in which case he was deluded; indeed, he was insane. That is the second possibility. The third possibility is that the claims were true. C. S. Lewis pointed out that, 'A man who was merely a man and said the sort of things Jesus said would not be a great moral teacher. He would either be insane or else he would be the devil of Hell... . You must make your choice,' he writes. Either Jesus was, and is, the Son of God or else he was insane or evil but, C. S. Lewis goes on, 'Let us not come up with any patronising nonsense

about His being a great human teacher. He has not left that
open to us. He did not intend to.'[179]

II. What evidence is there to support what he said?

In order to assess which of these three possibilities is right
we need to examine the evidence we have about his life.

1. His teaching

The teaching of Jesus is widely acknowledged to be the
greatest teaching that has ever fallen from human lips. The
Sermon on the Mount contains some supremely challenging
and radical teaching: 'Love your enemies' (Matthew 5:44);
'Turn the other cheek' (Matthew 5:39); 'Do to others as you
would have them do to you' (Luke 6:31).

John Mortimer, creator of the television series *Rumpole*,
explained why, although a long-term atheist, he now
describes himself as 'a leading member of the Atheists For
Christ Society'! Asked what brought about this change, he
said, 'Seeing the impact on society of a generation that has
rejected God and, as a result, Christian ethics. What is beyond
doubt,' he writes, 'Is that the Gospels provide a system of
ethics to which we must return if we are to avoid social
disasters'. The article was headed, 'Even the unbelievers
should go back to church today'.

Jesus' teaching is the foundation of our entire civilisation
in the West. Many of the laws in Europe were originally based
on his teaching. We are making progress in virtually every

field of science and technology. We travel faster and know more, and yet in the past 2,000 years no one has improved on the moral teaching of Jesus Christ.

Bernard Ramm, an American professor of theology, said this about the teachings of Jesus:

> They are read more, quoted more, loved more, believed more, and translated more because they are the greatest words ever spoken... . Their greatness lies in the pure lucid spirituality in dealing clearly, definitively, and authoritatively with the greatest problems that throb in the human breast... . No other man's words have the appeal of Jesus' words because no other man can answer these fundamental human questions as Jesus answered them. They are the kind of words and the kind of answers we would expect God to give.[180]

2. His works

To test the extraordinary claims Jesus made, it makes sense to look not only at what he said but also at what he did. Jesus said that the miracles he performed were in themselves evidence that 'the Father is in me, and I in the Father' (John 10:38). Jesus must have been the most extraordinary person to have around. Sometimes people say that Christianity is boring. Well, it was not boring being with Jesus. When he went to a party, he turned water into wine (John 2:1-11). He received one man's picnic and multiplied it so that it could feed thousands (Mark 6:30-44). He had control over the elements and could speak to the wind and the waves and thereby stop a storm (Mark 4:35-41). He carried out the most remarkable healings: opening blind eyes, causing the deaf and dumb to hear and speak and enabling the paralysed to walk again. When he visited a hospital, a man who had been an invalid for thirty-eight years was able to pick up his bed and walk (John 5:1-9). He set people free from evil forces which had dominated their lives. On occasions, he even brought those who had died back to life (John 11:38-44).

Yet it was not just his miracles that made his work so impressive. It was his love, especially for the loveless (such as the lepers and the prostitutes), which seemed to motivate all that he did. The supreme demonstration of his love for us was shown on the cross when he laid down his life 'for his friends'. Surely these are not the actions of an evil or deluded man? When he was in exile on St. Helena, Napoleon was reported as saying to one of his former generals, 'I know men, and I tell you that Jesus Christ was more than a man.... Everything in Christ astonishes me. His spirit overawes me, and His will confounds me. Between Him and whoever else in the world, there is no possible comparison.'[181]

3. His character

The character of Jesus has impressed millions who would not call themselves Christians. For example, Bernard Levin wrote of Jesus, 'Is not the nature of Christ, in the words of the New Testament, enough to pierce to the soul anyone with a soul to be pierced? ... he still looms over the world, his message still clear, his pity still infinite, his consolation still effective, his words still full of glory, wisdom and love'.[182]

Here was someone who exemplified supreme unselfishness but never self-pity; humility but not weakness; joy but never at another's expense; kindness but not indulgence. He was a person in whom even his enemies could find no fault and whose friends said he was without sin. It has been said that our character is truly tested when we are under pressure or in pain. When Jesus was being tortured, he said, 'Father, forgive them, for they do not know what they are doing' (Luke 22:34). Surely no one could suggest that such a man was evil or unbalanced?

4. His fulfilment of Old Testament prophecy

Wilbur Smith, the American writer on theological topics, said:

> The ancient world had many different devices for determining the future, known as divination, but not in the entire gamut of Greek and Latin literature, even though they used the words prophet and prophecy, can we find any real specific prophecy of a great historic event to come in the distant future, nor any prophecy of a Saviour to arrive in the human race ... Mohammedanism cannot point to any prophecies of the coming of Mohammed uttered hundreds of years before his birth. Neither can the founders of any cult in this country rightly identify any ancient text specifically foretelling their appearance.[183]

Yet in the case of Jesus, he fulfilled over 300 prophecies (spoken by different voices over 500 years), including twenty-nine major prophecies fulfilled in a single day – the day he died. Although some of these prophecies may have found fulfilment at one level in the prophet's own day, they found their ultimate fulfilment in Jesus Christ. I suppose it could be suggested that Jesus was a clever con man who deliberately set out to fulfil these prophecies in order to show that he was the Messiah foretold in the Old Testament. The problem with that suggestion is, first, the sheer number of them would have made it extremely difficult. Secondly, humanly speaking he had no control over many of the events. For example, the exact manner of his death was foretold in the Old Testament (Isaiah 53), the place of his burial and even the place of his birth (Micah 5:2). Suppose Jesus had been a con man wanting to fulfil all these prophecies. It would have been a bit late by the time he discovered the place in which he was supposed to have been born!

5. His Resurrection

The physical Resurrection from the dead of Jesus Christ is the cornerstone of Christianity. The atheist Richard Dawkins was correct when he said that, 'If the Resurrection is not true, Christianity becomes null and void'.[184] For myself, it was through the life, death and in particular the Resurrection of Jesus that I came to believe that there is a God. The New Testament theologian and Bishop of Durham, Tom Wright, said this, 'The Christian claim is not that Jesus is to be understood in terms of a God about whom we already know; it is this: the Resurrection of Jesus strongly suggests that the world has a Creator, and that that Creator is to be seen in terms of, through the lens of, Jesus'. But what is the evidence that the Resurrection really happened? I want to summarise the evidence under four main headings.

1. His absence from the tomb

Many theories have been put forward to explain the fact that Jesus' body was absent from the tomb on the first Easter Day, but none of them is very convincing. First, it has been suggested that Jesus did not die on the cross, but that he was still alive when he was put in the tomb and that he later recovered. But Mel Gibson's film, *The Passion*, made real the physical trauma of the Roman flogging which Jesus experienced. He was then nailed to a cross for six hours. Could a man in this condition push away a stone weighing probably a ton and a half? The soldiers were clearly convinced that he was dead or they would not have taken his body down from the cross. If they had allowed a prisoner to escape, they would have been liable to the death penalty. One New Testament scholar has joked that the only intriguing aspect of this theory is that it keeps coming back from the dead!

Furthermore, when the soldiers discovered that Jesus was already dead, 'One of the soldiers pierced Jesus' side with a spear, bringing a sudden flow of blood and water' (John 19:34). This appears to be the separation of clot and serum which we know today is strong medical evidence that Jesus was dead.[185] John did not write it for that reason; he would not have possessed that knowledge, which makes it even more powerful evidence that Jesus was indeed dead.

Secondly, some have suggested that the disciples stole the body and began a rumour that Jesus had risen from the dead. Leaving aside the fact that the tomb was guarded, this theory is psychologically improbable. The disciples were depressed and disillusioned at the time of Jesus' death. It would have needed something extraordinary to transform the apostle Peter from a dejected and despondent deserter into the man who preached so powerfully at Pentecost that 3,000 people were converted. In addition, when one considers how much they had to suffer for what they believed (floggings, torture, and for some even death), it seems inconceivable that they would be prepared to endure all that for something they knew to be untrue.

Thirdly, some have said that the authorities stole the body. This seems the least probable theory of all. If the authorities had stolen the body, why did they not produce it when they were trying to quash the rumour that Jesus had risen from the dead? Remember how quickly Iraqi television showed pictures of the body of Saddam Hussein after his execution? The authorities (both Jewish and Roman) would certainly have used all the many resources at their disposal to display Jesus' body publicly if they had actually been able to locate it. Perhaps the most fascinating piece of evidence relating to Jesus' absence from the tomb is John's description of the grave-clothes. In a way, the 'empty tomb' is a misnomer. When Peter and John went to the tomb they saw the grave-clothes which were, as the Christian apologist Josh McDowell put it in *The Resurrection Factor*, 'Like the empty chrysalis of a caterpillar's cocoon' – when the butterfly has emerged.[186] It was as if Jesus had simply passed through the grave-clothes. Not surprisingly, John 'saw and believed' (John 20:8).

2. His appearances to the disciples

Were these hallucinations? The Concise Oxford Dictionary describes a hallucination as an 'apparent perception of an external object not actually present'. Hallucinations normally occur in highly strung, highly imaginative and very nervous people, or in people who are sick or on drugs. The disciples do not fit into any of these categories. Burly fishermen, tax collectors and sceptics like Thomas are not likely candidates for mass hallucination experiences! Furthermore, people who hallucinate would be unlikely to suddenly stop doing so. Jesus appeared to his disciples on eleven different occasions over a period of six weeks and finally to Paul, 'As to one untimely born' (1 Cor. 15:8). The number of occasions and the sudden cessation make the hallucination theory highly improbable. Furthermore, over 500 people saw the risen Jesus. It is possible for one person to hallucinate. Maybe it is possible for two or three people to share the same hallucination. But is it likely that 500 people would all share the same hallucination? Finally, hallucinations are subjective. There is no objective reality – it is like seeing a ghost. Jesus could be touched, he ate a piece of grilled fish (Luke 24:42-43) and on one occasion he cooked breakfast for the disciples (John 21:1-14). Peter says, '[They] ate and drank with him after he rose from the dead' (Acts 10:41). He held long conversations with them, teaching them many things about the Kingdom of God (Acts 1:3).

3. The immediate effect

Jesus' rising from the dead, as one would expect, had a dramatic impact on the world. The church was born and grew at a tremendous rate. As Michael Green, writer of many popular and scholarly works, puts it:

[The] church … beginning from a handful of uneducated fishermen and tax gatherers, swept across the whole known world in the next three hundred years. It is a perfectly amazing story of peaceful revolution that has no parallel in the history of the world. It came about because Christians were able to say to inquirers, 'Jesus did not only die for you. He is alive! You can meet him and discover for yourself the reality we are talking about!' They did, and they joined the church and the church, born from that Easter grave, spread everywhere.[187]

4. Christian experience

Countless millions of people down the ages have experienced the risen Jesus Christ. They consist of people of every colour, race, tribe, continent and nationality. They come from different economic, social and intellectual backgrounds. To use the words of Desmond Tutu, Christians are the 'rainbow people of God', all united in a common experience of the risen Jesus Christ.

Millions of Christians all over the world today enjoy this experience. Over the years I have also experienced that Jesus Christ is alive today. I have experienced his love, his power and the reality of a relationship which convinces me that he really is alive. Sherlock Holmes said, 'When you have eliminated the impossible, whatever remains, however improbable, must be the truth'.[188] When we looked earlier in the chapter at what Jesus said about himself, we saw that there were only three realistic possibilities – either he was and is the Son of God, or else deluded or something more sinister. When one looks at the evidence it does not make sense to say that he was insane or evil. The whole weight of his teaching, his works, his character, his fulfilment of Old Testament prophecy and his conquest of death make those suggestions absurd, illogical and unbelievable. On the other hand, they lend the strongest possible support to Jesus' own self-understanding as a man whose identity was God.

In conclusion, as C. S. Lewis pointed out, 'We are faced then with a frightening alternative'. Either Jesus was (and is) exactly what he said, or else he was insane or something worse. To C. S. Lewis, it seemed clear that he could have been neither insane nor evil and thus he concludes, 'However strange or terrifying or unlikely it may seem, I have to accept the view that he was and is God'.[189]

Endnotes

One: Has Science Disproved God?

1   Terry Eagleton, 'Lunging, Flailing, Mispunching' (Review of *The God Delusion*), p.1; Sam Harris, *Letter to a Christian Nation* (Bantam Press, 2007), p.47.

2   Richard Dawkins, *The Root of All Evil* – part 1: 'The God Delusion'.

3   Richard Dawkins, *The God Delusion* (Black Swan, 2007), p.308.

4   Ibid., p.317.

5   Harris, *Letter to a Christian Nation*, p.87.

6   There is a net growth of over 20,000 new Christians added to the church every single day (77 million increase in the last decade). Source taken from *World Christian Encyclopaedia* (Oxford University Press, inc. USA).

7   Friedrich Nietzsche, *The Gay Science*, Section 125, tr. Walter Kaufmann.

8   Dawkins, *The God Delusion*, p.5.

9   Roger Scruton, *The Oxford Dictionary of Epistemology*.

10 Dawkins, *The God Delusion*, p.5.

11 Ibid.

12 Dawkins, *The Root of All Evil* – part 1.

13 C. S. Lewis, *Miracles* (Fontana, 1947), p.110.

14 Lesley Newbigin, *Foolishness to the Greeks* (SPCK, 1986), p.71.

15 John Polkinghorne, *One World* (SPCK, 1986), p.1.

16 Herbert Butterfield, *The Origins of Modern Science 1300 -1800* (The Free Press, 1957).

17 Dawkins, *The Root of All Evil* – part 1.

18 Richard Dawkins, 'The God Delusion' debate with John Lennox, 3 October, 2007, Birmingham, Alabama.

19 Ibid.

20 Ibid.

21 Ibid., p.88.

22 Dawkins, *The God Delusion*, p.99.

23 Ibid.

24 John Cornwell, *Darwin's Angel – An Angelic Riposte To 'The God Delusion'* (Profile Books, 2007), pp.16-17.

25 Michael Atiyah, *Creating a Statue of James Clerk Maxwell* (The Royal Society of Edinburgh, 2007).

26 Francis Collins, *The Language of God – A Scientist Presents Evidence for Belief* (Pocket Books, 2007), p.4.

27 Ibid., p.4.

28 Dawkins, *The God Delusion*, p.99.

29 Collins, *The Language of God*, p.6.

30 Francis Collins, speech at the National Prayer Breakfast, Washington, DC, 1 February 2007.

31 *Borrowed Light: Hymn Texts, Prayers and Poems* (Oxford University Press, 2004).

32 Dawkins, *The Root of All Evil* – part 1.

33 David Hume, *On Miracles* (1748), p.114.

34 Max Planck, *A Scientific Autobiography* (Williams and Norgate,1950), p.155.

35 Lewis, *Miracles*, p.51.

36 David Atkinson, *The Wings of Refuge* (Inter Varsity Press, 1893), p.13.

37 Stephen Hawking, *Black Holes and Baby Universes and Other Essays* (Bantam Press, 1993).

38 For the original version of this story see John Lennox, *God's Undertaker – Has Science Buried God?* (Lion Hudson PLC, 2007), pp.40-41.

39 Ibid.

40 Harris, *Letter to a Christian Nation*, pp.62-63.

41 Stephen J. Gould, 'Impeaching a Self-Appointed Judge' (review of Phillip Johnson's *Dawin on Trial*), *Scientific American*, 267 (1992), pp.1180-21.

42 Collins, *The Language of God*, p.6.

43 Ibid., p.167.

44 *Science, Philosophy and Religion, A Symposium* (New York, 1941).

45 John Houghton, 'Big Science, Big God', *The John Ray Initiative*, JRI Briefing Paper No 15, pp.4-5.

46 Ibid.

47 Science, *Scientia,* knowledge – 'The state or fact of knowing,' *New Shorter English Dictionary.*

48 This question, 'Why is there something rather than nothing?' was asked by the German philosopher and mathematician, Godfrey Liebniz.

49 Harris, *Letter to a Christian Nation*, pp.73-74.

50   Dawkins, *The Root of All Evil* – part 1.

51   Cornwell, *Darwin's Angel*, p.151.

52   Alistair McGrath with Joanna Collicut McGrath, *The Dawkins Delusion?* (SPCK, 2007), p.10.

53   Peter Medawar, *The Limits of Science* (Oxford University Press, 1985), p.66.

54   Collins, *The Language of God*, p.67.

55   Ibid., p.165.

56   Stephen Hawking, *The Times*, 6 September 1993.

57   Polkinghorne, *One World*, p.57.

58   Stephen Hawking, *A Brief History of Time* (New York, Bantam Press, 1998) p.63.

59   Dawkins, *The God Delusion*, p.141.

60   See Ibid., pp.145-147.

61   Ibid., p.354.

62   J. John, *Life Means What?* (Hodder & Stoughton), p.13.

63   Humphrys, *In God We Doubt*, pp.280-1.

64   Ibid., p.321-2.

65   Ibid., p.310-1.

Two: Does Religion Do more Harm Than Good?

66   J. B. Philipps, *Gathered Gold* (Evangelical Press, 1984).

67   Tobias Jones, 'Secular fundamentalists are the new totalitarians,' *The Guardian* (Saturday 6 January 2007).

68   Richard Dawkins, 'Is Science a Religion?' *The Humanist*, 57 (1997), pp.26-29.

69   C. S. Lewis, *Mere Christianity,* (Fount, 1952), p.39.

70 Collins, *The Language of God*, p.231.

71 Richard Dawkins, *The God Delusion*, p.248.

72 Ibid., p.31.

73 Humphrys, *In God We Doubt*, p.145.

74 Alvin Plantinga.

75 Thomas Paine, *Age of Reason* (1795), quoted in Brian McLaren, *Everything Must Change* (Nelson Books, 2008), p.157.

76 McGrath, *The Dawkins Delusion?*, p.53.

77 This is not a book on hermeneutics (that is how to interpret the Bible); however, for further reading, see John Goldingay, *Approaches to Old Testament Interpretation* (Updated ed.: Apollos, 1990), Goldingay, *How to Read the Bible* (Triangle, 1997), Christopher J. H. Wright, *Knowing Jesus through the Old Testament* (Monarch Books, 2005, 1992).

78 For further reading, see Amy Orr-Ewing, *Why Trust The Bible?* (Inter-Varsity Press, 2005), p.92 and John W. Wenham, *The Enigma of Evil – Can we believe in the goodness of God?* (Inter-Varsity Press, 1985), pp.13-16.

79 Nicholas Lash 'Where Does The God Delusion Come From?' *New Blackfriars Magazine*, p.513.

80 Dawkins, *The God Delusion*, p.253.

81 Christopher Hitchens, *God Is Not Great: How Religion Poisons Everything* (Hachette Book Group USA, 2007), p.213.

82 Alister McGrath and Christopher Hitchens Debate, 12 October 2007, Georgetown, USA.

83 Dawkins writes that, 'DNA neither cares nor knows. DNA just is. And we dance to its music.' In Dawkins', *River out of Eden: A Darwinian View of Life* (Phoenix, 1996), p.155.

84 The 'God-shaped hole' is wrongly attributed to Sartre. It should be Blaise Pascal.

85 Rod Liddle, *Sunday Times* (8 October 2006).

86 Afterword by Richard Dawkins in John Brockmas (ed.), *What Is Your Dangerous Idea?* (Pocket Books, 2007), p.308.

87 In a section entitled 'When it is wrong not to have an abortion' in Chapter 11, 'Abortion Reconsidered' in Jonathan Glover, *Causing Death and Saving Lives* (Penguin, London, 1977), reprinted 1990, p.146.

88 'New-born babies, like foetuses are replaceable. It is wrong to kill a baby who has a good chance of having a worth-while life, but in terms of this objection, it would not be wrong to kill him if the alternative to his existence was the existence of someone else with an equally good chance of a life at least as worthwhile (Ibid, *Causing Death* and *Saving Lives*, p.158-9).

89 Jacqueline Worswick, *A House Called Helen- The development of hospice care for children* (Oxford University Press, 2000), pp.73-74.

90 Dawkins, *Is Science a Religion?*, pp.26-29.

91 Ibid.

92 Ibid., p.295.

93 Keith Ward, *Is Religion Dangerous?* (Lion Hudson PLC, 2006), p.74.

94 Dawkins, *The God Delusion*, p.278.

95 Humphrys, *In God We Doubt*, p.287.

96 Ibid., p.293.

97 Cornwell *Darwin's Angel*, p.90.

98 Michael Bourdeaux, *Patriarch and Prophets: Persecution of the Russian Orthodox Church* (Mowbrays, 1975), p.38.

99 Dawkins, *The God Delusion*, p.273.

100 Ibid.

101 McGrath, *The Dawkins Delusion?*, p.48.

102 Dawkins, *The God Delusion*, p.292.

103 Richard Dawkins on his collection of essays, *The Devil's Chaplain* – interview by Laura Sheahen.

104 Ibid., p.271.

105 Ibid.

106 Financial Times Review of Hitchens, *Financial Times Magazine* (23/24 June, 2007).

107 Ibid.

108 Humphrys, *In God We Doubt*, p.217; Ibid., p.232; Ibid., p.322.

109 Charlie Mackesy, talk given at HTB on 6 January, 2008.

110 Ward, *Is Religion Dangerous?*, p.157.

111 Richard Dawkins 'The God Delusion' debate with John Lennox, 3 October, 2007.

112 Dawkins, *The God Delusion*, p.317.

113 Richard Dawkins, *A Devil's Chaplain – Selected Essays* (Orion House, 2003), p.283.

114 Ibid., p.284-6.

Three: Is Faith irrational?

115 Dawkins, *The Root of all Evil* – part 2, 'The Virus of Faith'.

116 Richard Dawkins, *The Selfish Gene* (Oxford University Press, 2006), p.198.

117 Richard Dawkins, *The God Delusion*, p.5.

118 Richard Dawkins, *The Root of All Evil* Bonus DVD – Galapagos Islands, May 2007.

119 Albert Einstein, *Ideas and Opinions* (1973), p.233.

120 Amy Orr-Ewing, *Why Trust the Bible? Answers To Tough Questions* (Inter-Varsity Press, 2005), pp.113-114.

121 Michael Ruse, *The Evolution-Creation Struggle*, pp. 4, 287, quoted in Nicholas Lash 'Where Does The God Delusion Come From?' *New Blackfriars Magazine*, p.521.

122 The conversation is reported in John Dominic Crossan, *The Dark Interval: Towards A Theology of Story* (1975), p.31.

123 *The Times*, 9 October 2007, p.55.

124 Quoted in Lash, 'Where Does The God Delusion Come From?', p.512.

125 John Paul II, *Fides et Ratio – Encyclical Letter of Pope John Paul II* (Catholic Trust Society, 1998), p.50.

126 Dawkins, *A Devil's Chaplain*, p.288-9 (emphasis added).

127 John Paul II, *Fides et Ratio*, p.73.

128 Ibid., p.3.

129 Father Raniero Cantalamessa, *Sober Intoxication of the Spirit – Filled with the Fullness of God* (Servant Books, St. Anthony Messenger Press, 2005), p.99.

130 Blaise Pascal, *The Pensées: Thoughts, letters and minor works*, Section VII, 430.

131 Dawkins, *The Root of All Evil*, Galapagos Islands

132 Collins, *The Language of God*, p.66.

133 Stephen Hawking, *A Brief History of Time. From the Big Bang to Black Holes* (Bantam Press, 1988), p.46.

134 Robert Jastrow, *God and the Astronomers* (W. W. Norton, 1992), pp.107, 14.

135 Lesslie Newbigin, *Foolishness to the Greeks* (SPCK, 2001) p.72.

136 Paul Badham, *Church Times* (26 October 2007).

137 Roger Penrose, *The Emperor's New Mind* (Oxford University Press, 1989), pp.445-6.

138 Houghton, *Big Science, Big God*, p.3.

139 Ibid.

140 Ibid.

141 David Hume, 1738, reference unkown.

142 St. Augustine, *Confessions*, Book 1, Section 1.

143 By kind permission of Bernard Levin.

144 Dawkins, *The God Delusion*, p.191.

145 Alistair McGrath, *The Dawkins Delusion?* p.28.

146 Collins, *The Language of God*, p.37.

147 Blaise Pascal, *The Penses: Thoughts, letters and minor works*, Section VII, p.425.

148 John Stott, *Authentic Christianity* (Intervarsity Press, 1996), p.47.

149 Dawkins, *The God Delusion*, p.97.

150 The Roman historian Tacitus, concerning the 'Great Fire of Rome' in *Annals*, book 15, chapter 44 (c.116), p.44.

151 Summary from John Young with David Wilkinson, *The Case Against Christ* (Hodder & Stoughton, 2006), p.148.

152 Dawkins, *The God Delusion*, p.93.

153 Ibid., p.95.

154 Ibid., p.97.

155 In an interview given to the *Saturday Evening Post*, 26 October 1929 quoted in, *Einstein and Religion: physics and theology*, by Max Jammer (Princeton University Press, 1999).

156 See, for instance, *Jesus and the Eyewitnesses*, by Richard Bauckham (Eerdmans, 2006) and, *The Historical Reliability of the Gospels*, by Craig Blomberg (forthcoming).

157 Ibid.

158 N. T. Wright, *The Resurrection of the Son of God* (Fortress Press, 2003), p.710.

159 Dawkins, *The God Delusion*, p.253.

160 Lord Lyttleton, *Observations of the Conversion and Apostleship of St. Paul*, (1747).

161 From the Francis Collins 'National Prayer Breakfast', 1 February 2007, Washington, D. C.

162 Attributed to C. S. Lewis.

163 Aleksandr Solzhenitsyn, *The Gulag Archipelago 1918-1956*, (1973).

164 Graham Tomlin, *A Theologian's Perspective*, p.106.

Postscript – A Theologians Perspective

165 D. Allen, *Christian Belief in a Postmodern World: The Full Wealth of Conviction* (Westminster / John Knox, 1989), p.180.

166 Dawkins, *The God Delusion*, p.369; Ibid., p.374.

167 Ibid., p.79.

168 Ibid., p.103.

169 Ibid., pp.130-2.

170 Pascal, *The Pensées: Thoughts, letters and minor works*.

Appendix – Who Is Jesus?

171 M. Amis, *Koba the Dread: Laughter and the Twenty Million* (Jonathan Cape, 2007), p.116.

172 Josephus, *Antiquities*, XVIII 63f. Even if, as some suggest, the text has been corrupted, none the less the evidence of Josephus confirms the historical existence of Jesus.

173 F. J. A. Hort, *The New Testament in the Original Greek*, Vol. I (Macmillan), p.561.

174 Sir Frederic Kenyon, *The Bible and Archaeology* (Harper and Row, 1940).

175 In an interview given to the *Saturday Evening Post*, 26 October 1929 (quoted in, *Einstein and Religion: physics and theology*, by Max Jammer (Princeton University Press, 1999)).

176 See, for instance, *Jesus and the Eyewitnesses*, by Richard Bauckham (Eerdmans, 2006) and, *The Historical Reliability of the Gospels*, by Craig Blomberg (forthcoming).

177 Jean-Jacques Rousseau, *Emile: Or Treatise on Education* (Prometheus, 2003).

178 C. S. Lewis, *Mere Christianity* (Fount, 1952).

179 Ibid.

180 Bertram Ramm, *Protestant Christian Evidence* (Moody Press).

181 In conversation with Comte H.G. Bertrand (quoted in *The Life of Napoleon*, by John Abbot (Kessinger, 2005)).

182 By kind permission of Bernard Levin.

183 Wilbur Smith, *The Incomparable Book* (Beacon Publications, 1961).

184 Quoted in *The Spectator*, 15 April 2006.

185 A team of medical experts produced a detailed study of the physical effects of the treatment which Jesus' body was made to endure based on such circumstantial details and concluded that as a result of hypovolemic shock and exhaustion asphyxia, it would have been a medical impossibility for Jesus to have been alive when he was taken down from the cross (there is a report of

the study in *Journal of the American Medical Association*, Vol. 255, 21 March 1986).

186 Josh McDowell, *The Resurrection Factor* (Here's Life Publishers).

187 Michael Green, *Man Alice* (Inter Varsity Press, 1968).

188 *The Sign of Four* by Sir Arthur Conan Doyle (Penguin Classics, 2001).

189 C. S. Lewis, *Surprised By Joy* (Fontana, 1952).